Documents and Debates
Twentieth-Century Europe

Documents and Debates
General Editor: John Wroughton M.A., F.R.Hist.S.

Twentieth-Century Europe

Richard Brown
Houghton Regis Upper School, Bedfordshire

Christopher Daniels
Royal Latin School, Buckingham

Macmillan Education
London and Basingstoke

First published 1981

Reprinted 1982

Published by
MACMILLAN EDUCATION LIMITED
Houndmills Basingstoke Hampshire RG21 2XS
and London
Associated companies throughout the world

Printed in Hong Kong

British Library Cataloguing in Publication Data

Brown, Richard
    Twentieth century Europe. – (Documents and
    debates).
    1. Europe – History – 20th century
    I. Title   II. Daniels, Christopher   III. Series
    940.5   D424
    ISBN 0–333–27984–0

Contents

General Editor's Preface

This book forms part of a series entitled *Documents and Debates*, which is aimed primarily at the sixth form. Each volume covers approximately one century of either British or European history and consists of up to ten sections, each dealing with a major theme. In most cases a varied selection of documents will bring evidence to bear on the chosen theme, supplemented by a stimulating extract from a modern historian. A few 'Debate' sections, however, will centre on the most important controversies of each century. Here extracts from the changing opinions of modern research, normally found only in learned journals and expensive monographs, will be made available in manageable form. The series intends partly to provide experience for those pupils who are required to answer questions on documentary extracts at 'A' Level, and partly to provide pupils of all abilities with a digestible and interesting collection of source material, which will extend the normal textbook approach.

This book is designed essentially for the pupil's own personal use. The authors' introduction will put the century as a whole into perspective, highlighting the central issues, main controversies, available source material and recent developments. Although it is clearly not our intention to replace the traditional textbook, each section will carry its own brief introduction, which will set the documents into context. The short, select bibliography is intended to encourage the pupil to follow up issues raised in the section by further reading – without being subjected to the off-putting experience of an exhaustive list. A wide variety of source material has been used in order to give the pupils the maximum amount of experience – letters, speeches, newspapers, memoirs, diaries, official papers, Acts of Parliament, Minute Books, accounts, local documents, family papers etc. The questions vary in difficulty, but aim throughout to compel the pupil to think in depth by the use of unfamiliar material. Historical knowledge and understanding will be tested, as well as basic comprehension. Pupils will also be encouraged by the questions to assess the reliability of evidence, to recognise bias and emotional prejudice, to reconcile conflicting accounts and to extract the essential from the irrelevant. Some questions, marked with an asterisk, require knowledge outside the immediate extract and are intended for further research or discussion, based on the pupil's general knowledge of the period. Finally, we hope the students using this material will learn something of the nature of historical inquiry and the role of the historian.

John Wroughton

Acknowledgements

The authors and publishers wish to thank the following who have kindly given permission for the use of copyright material:

St Antony's College, Oxford, and Sir Max Beloff for an extract from *St Antony's Papers No. 5: The Decline of The Third Republic*;

Associated Book Publishers Ltd for extracts from *Revolutions and Peace Treaties 1917–1920* by Gerhard Schulz, translated by Marion Jackson, published by Methuen & Co., and from *The Nazi Seizure of Power* by William Sheridan Allen, published by Eyre & Spottiswoode (Publishers) Ltd;

The Bodley Head for extracts from *Lenin in Zurich* and *August 1914* by Alexander Solzhenitsyn, and from *The Great Wall of France* by Vivien Rowe, published by Putnam & Co. Ltd;

Ernest Benn Ltd for an extract from *The Germans at Versailles 1919* translated by Geoffrey Dunlop;

Cambridge University Press for extracts from *The Social and Political Doctrines of Contemporary Europe* translated by Michael Oakeshott, and *Power and the Pursuit of Peace: Theory and Practice in the History of Relations between States* by F. S. Hisley (1963);

Jonathan Cape Ltd for an extract from *The Slump: Society and Politics during the Depression* by John Stevenson and Chris Cook;

Cassell Ltd for extracts from *The Second World War* and *Sinews of Peace – Post-War Speeches* by Winston S. Churchill; extract from *The Memoirs: Facing the Dictators* by the Earl of Avon;

Librairie Armand Colin, Paris, for an extract from *l'Allemagne de Weimar 1918–1933* by G. Castellan edited by A. Colin;

Curtis Brown Ltd on behalf of Christopher Isherwood for an extract from *Mr Norris Changes Trains*;

Andre Deutsch Ltd for an extract from *Khruschev Remembers* Vol. 1 by N. Khruschev;

Farrar, Straus & Giroux Inc. for an extract from *Mr President* by William Hillman;

Faber & Faber Ltd for extracts from *The Revolution Betrayed* by Leon Trotsky;

Librairie Ernest Flammarion, Paris, for an extract from *Jadis II, d'Une Guerre a l'Autre 1914–1936* by E. Herriot;

Michael J. Florinsky for an extract from *The End of the Russian Empire* (1976);

Fontana Paperbacks Ltd for an extract from *Britain and the World Economy 1919–1970* by L. J. Williams;

Elaine Green Ltd on behalf of Richard M. Watt for an extract from *The Kings Depart – The Tragedy of Germany: Versailles and the German Revolution*, copyright © Richard M. Watt 1968, 1971;

Hamish Hamilton Ltd for an extract from *The Origins of the Second World War* by A. J. P. Taylor;

Harvard University Press for an extract from *How Russia is Ruled* by Merle Fainsod, copyright © 1953, 1963 by the President and Fellows of Harvard College;

A. M. Heath & Co. Ltd on behalf of the George Orwell Estate and Mrs Sonia Brownell Orwell for an extract from *The Road to Wigan Pier* published by Martin Secker & Warburg Ltd;

The Controller of Her Majesty's Stationery Office for an extract from *The Hossbach*

Memorandum – Documents on German Foreign Policy 1918–1945 – Series D, Vol. 1;
William Heinemann Ltd for an extract from *English Journey* by J. B. Priestley;
David Higham Associates Ltd on behalf of Malcolm Muggeridge for an extract from *Ciano's Diary*;

Hodder & Stoughton Ltd for an extract from *Failure of a Mission*, Berlin 1937–1939 by Sir Nevile Henderson (1940);

Hutchinson Publishing Group Ltd for an extract from *Mein Kampf* by Adolf Hitler;

Lawrence & Wishart Ltd for an extract from the *Selected Works* of Lenin (1975);

Martin Secker & Warburg Ltd for extracts from *Lenin and the Bolsheviks* by Adam B. Ullam;

New Left Review for extracts from 'The Question of Stalin' by Lucio Colletti, *New Left Review 61* (1970);

Oxford University Press for extracts from *The Politics of the Prussian Army 1640–1945* by C. A. Craig (1955) and *English History 1914–1945* by A. J. P. Taylor (1965);

The Past and Present Society, and Dr T. W. Mason, for an extract from *Some Origins of the Second World War* published in *Past and Present* No. 29 (December 1964);

Penguin Books Ltd for an extract from *An Economic History of the U.S.S.R.* by A. Nave (1976);

Random House Inc. for an extract from *Europe Since Napoleon* (2nd edition, revised) by D. Thompson;

Routledge & Kegan Paul Ltd for extracts from *Italian Foreign Policy 1870–1940* by C. J. Lowe and F. Marzari;

D. Mack Smith for an extract from *Mussolini as a Military Leader* (Stenton Lecture, University of Reading 1963);

Maurice Temple Smith Ltd for an extract from *Too Serious a Business: European Armed Forces and the Approach to the Second World War* by D. C. Watt (1975);

Weidenfeld & Nicholson Ltd for an extract from *Inside the Third Reich* by Albert Speer;

Every effort has been made to trace all the copyright holders but if any have been inadvertently overlooked the publishers will be pleased to make the necessary arrangement at the first opportunity.

The cover illustration is reproduced by courtesy of the Tate Gallery, London.

Europe in the Twentieth Century

The Nature of Evidence

Today historians and all interested in the study of history take great pains to emphasise and assert the integrity of their discipline. They also state that their subject is much more exacting and complex than often appears to those viewing it from outside. Gone is the optimism which Lord Acton characterised when he believed, at the beginning of this century, that the attainment of full historical knowledge was in the grasp of the profession. This optimism has been replaced by a greater realism about both the character of the subject and the problems implicit in its study. Both in the teaching of history and in research in universities and colleges great advances have been made in techniques, especially in the framing and posing of questions, and the realisation that questions may not be capable of definitive answer. This has been paralleled in the collection, collation and assessment of historical evidence and especially in the relationship between the evidence and the questions which it can properly be expected to answer.

In the search for 'total' history — which may be defined as an attempt to achieve complete empathy with a specific period — the historian now divides his studies somewhat at peril into social, economic, constitutional, diplomatic or political categories. History is in the process of being liberated from the constraints of the nineteenth and early twentieth centuries. Some historians have embraced ideology as a tool in making the past explicable, much to the chagrin of their more conservative colleagues. Just how far ideology is a better methodological technique for the historian is certainly a matter of controversy. History can very easily become the tool of ideology as both German writing in the 1930s and Soviet scholarship since 1917 show. The student needs to consider just how valuable is the emphasis on ideology in modern historical writing. Ideology's main danger for the historian is its insistence on the definitiveness of its answers. This seems to negate what is one of the central characteristics of history: its contrariness.

The renaissance in historical studies is particularly evident in the historian writing about the nineteenth and twentieth centuries. Perhaps this is because ideology has played such an important role in these centuries. This collection of documents is a selection taken exclusively from written or printed sources. A broad range of evidential material has not been included – cartoons, buildings, oral evidence, photographs, newsreel footage. This may be a major omission since all the topics could have been dealt with using visual evidence. The reader should ask why the nine themes have been chosen and whether the material presented either affects the conclusions reached or determines them.

The historian, analysing his discipline, must continually question the truths of statements made by his fellows. It is necessary to consider what it means to actually know something, the authority upon which the truth is based, and the evidence for or against a particular truth. Consider the following four truths:

1 I know that the angles of a triangle add up to 180 degrees.
2 I know that the buildings before me were built in the inter-war period.
3 I know that God exists.
4 I know that the food I am eating is steak.

In two cases – the first and the third – the idea of evidence is inappropriate. The first statement is an example of a conclusion from assumed premises. The third can only be tenable through personal revelation and cannot be tested in any deductive or empirical sense. By contrast, background knowledge of a relevant nature, the formulation of hypotheses and observation are essential to the second and fourth questions.

This exercise tells us that evidence means different things in different circumstances. There is no way in which historical evidence could be subjected to the scrutiny of scientific inquiry since there are no assumed premises in history. Similarly personal revelation plays no logical part in the analysis of material, though sometimes understanding of a historical phenomenon comes as in a flash of light.

The strength of historical knowledge gains in coherence from its three-part structure, as does any area of knowledge. These three elements are

1 the factual basis of knowledge e.g. 'I *know that* Hitler became chancellor of Germany in 1933.'
2 the methodological nature of knowledge e.g. 'I *know how* to examine Hitler's rise to power in Germany.'
3 the conceptual nature of knowledge e.g. 'I have a *general* understanding of the reasons behind the development of dictatorships in the twentieth century.'

The historian uses all of these aspects of knowledge to produce his rounded view of the past. To 'know' something on good authority (element 1) means that the thing that is 'known' – in this case that Hitler became chancellor of Germany in 1933 – is the outcome of an inquiry which has satisfied certain methodological criteria (element 2). The historian's generalised understanding of his subject provides him with the matrix he needs to formulate hypotheses and to know what questions to ask. This conceptual element is vague in character but is still of vital importance to the successful historian. It evolves gradually as a result of the analysis and selection of events. Once achieved, it can be turned around and used as the basis for historical study – e.g. 'I have a conceptual understanding of the effects of economic depression and unemployment. How does this help me in my understanding of Hitler's rise to power in the thirties?'

All good historical writing contains all three elements. For the historian of the twentieth century it is not always possible to use them in a completely precise manner. The impact of ideology on history means that the methodological slant of writing may be partial. The closer the events being discussed are to the historian the more difficult it is for him to appreciate their totality given the sheer weight of evidence – a physical problem given the output of many governmental agencies – and the difficulty of formulating the correct questions for it. It is even difficult to know what actually happened; the Kennedy assassination in 1963 is a very clear example.

The student of history has to take all these points into account: to wade through the plethora of evidence available, seek out the bias, examine the misleading or the misquoted. Then it is possible to understand the varying ideological stances the historian can take. Only then can the historian pose the proper sort of question about the recent past.

The Character of an Age

In his introduction to *The Last of Old Europe* – a photographic interpretation of the period 1848–1914 – A. J. P. Taylor emphasised the gulf that separates us from the people of Europe before the First World War. The effects of two European civil wars and the advent of conflicting totalitarian ideologies, the fruition of nationalism and the demise of imperialism, and the coming of age of the common man have transformed the nature of daily life for the 'submerged nine-tenths'. Science and technology (beyond the scope of this book) have similarly contributed to the twentieth century, at the apparent cost of religion. As Donald Watt wrote:

> it has been suggested that pre-1914 Europe partook of the nature of a society in five respects: the power relationships between its states; the rules and conventions which governed their behaviour one to another; the social relationships between their élites; the shared culture; and the common moralities of largely Christian states and peoples.

'War', Trotsky said, 'is the locomotive of history'. The First World War had a profound impact on all who survived it or who learned of it second-hand; in December 1938, during a speech to the Foreign Press Association, Neville Chamberlain, referring to the British people's emotions at the time of Munich, said that 'in imagination they saw husbands, brothers, and sons torn from their families, perhaps never to return; they saw their homes wrecked, their children terrified or mutilated, their happiness and peace of mind gone for ever'. The cemeteries and memorials like Tyne Cot, Hill 62, the Menin Gate and Thiepval were still fresh in many minds; in France the war had devastated the country materially just as the pre-war Dreyfus affair had dealt body-blows to her social and political structure. The consequences of the war for France were a weakness in manpower, an obsession with security and a fatal belief in static defences. For Italy and Germany, victor and vanquished, the war spelt the ruin of democracy (paradoxically so in Germany's case), totalitarian groups profiting from wartime enthusiasm and camaraderie, and post-war depression. The peace treaties signed in Paris in 1919 must bear a heavy burden for the post-war problems in the defeated and victorious nations, and for the long-term causes of the Second World War. In Russia, the war brought the Soviets to power, arguably the most significant event in the history of modern Europe.

The growth of totalitarian régimes in Europe between the wars fully deserves the five chapters given to it. Fascism and Communism were much closer in their political systems than their ideologies suggested — there was little to choose between the extermination of Kulaks and Jews, or between Katyn and Auschwitz. The failure of democratic governments in Italy and Germany to find a positive response to extremism or apathy has a significance for the future of democracy in some European countries today. Fascism, however, was a product of the 1920s and has few contemporary manifestations in a similar format. Its unperceived element was expansionism, a fact that even some latter-day historians have failed to recognise. Space has precluded sections on the Spanish Civil War or the efforts of the League of Nations, both important features of the inter-war period.

Even a slight reading of Flora Thompson's *Lark Rise to Candleford* or *Joseph Ashby of Tysoe* by Mabel Ashby reveals the changes of the present century on life for the majority of the population of Europe. These changes are a recent phenomenon, as an examination of the inter-war depression reminds us. They vary, of course, from country to country and from region to region, but the material well-being of most Europeans has improved at the same time as the political influence of Europe in the world has diminished with the advent of the superpowers: the USA and the USSR. The relationship of these two countries immediately after the Second World War is indicated in the section on the origins of the Cold War; few prophetic utterances have been as dramatically or chillingly realised as Churchill's 'iron curtain' speech in Fulton, Missouri. The perspective of the 1980s does not suggest any slackening in the tension between NATO and the Warsaw Pact, Europe being the scene for a third World War in Sir John Hackett's conception of the mid-1980s.

Study of the major personalities of this period of European history covers a vast range of human characteristics. Judging from the sections in this book it may seem that history is more concerned with knaves (to use Sir John Wheeler-Bennett's categorisation) than fools or heroes. Further reading should dispel this notion, as should investigation of the attempts to preserve Europe by peaceful or defensive means. The paradoxical result by 1945 was a divided Europe and the end of European worldwide hegemony.

I Versailles – A Settlement or a Fiasco?

Introduction

In the nineteenth century the function of a peace treaty was to resolve the differences between the protagonists and, where possible, to restore the status quo. There may have been some territorial rearrangement but nothing of a major nature. 1919 was different. Versailles was a settlement which attempted to resolve on the one hand *all* the problems posed by Germany and, on the other, to satisfy demands that she should be 'squeezed until the pips squeaked'.

The Great War was fought with a vehemence and horror it is difficult to imagine today. Technology brought killing to a level of sophistication most people thought was unbelievable. The illusion of heroic combat gave way to the reality of mud and machine guns, barbed wire and trenches. The Great War was viewed as 'the war to end all wars' and the Versailles settlement reflected this overwhelming desire for a secure peace. Why then did things go so wrong? Lloyd George, Clemenceau and Wilson were all intelligent men who were aware that peace was not going to be an easy thing to achieve. Lloyd George and Wilson were, for different reasons, sure that the war did mark a great discontinuity and that the peace settlement must reflect new realities not the pre-war ones. This Lloyd George made clear in his Fontainebleau memorandum of March 1919, and Wilson in his Fourteen Points. This section concentrates on the position of Germany in the immediate post-war period, and upon the illusions and the realities of peace.

The real desire to end wars for all time is reflected in the extract from Lord Robert Cecil's 1916 Memorandum. He feared the total collapse of the European system if war broke out again and proposed a dual system of arbitration and conference to prevent this eventuality. It was, however, an ideal which was not to be of sufficient force to stem either the reality of the peace treaty or the caution expressed by Lloyd George. It was a well-meaning but ultimately fruitless expedient.

Germany had been economically weakened by the war and was now compelled to accept a 'peace without honour'. It was assigned blame for the outbreak of the war in the treaty and had no option but to sign the document. Paul Löbe's speech to the Weimar Assembly in 1919 made clear the attitude of many Germans to the peace and contained the seeds for further discontent. Like Lloyd George, Löbe argued that the peace should take into account the growing strength of the working classes of Europe. Unlike him Löbe did not see the treaty fulfilling this. To him the treaty was essentially a conservative measure.

Richard Watt looks at the question from the other side. He examines three ideas: that peace was made necessary for Germany because of 'the stab in the back' by the revolutionary groups; that peace was unnecessary as the German army could have still won the war; that Versailles was only accepted by the militarists because it gave them the opportunity to live to fight another day.

These different views of the Versailles settlement are shown by G. Schulz to be a consequence of the failure of the peacemakers to consider 'all relevant issues', and their unwillingness to accept that revision of the settlement was essential if a just and lasting peace was to be achieved.

Versailles was one answer to the problems that existed for Europe in 1919. Hindsight allows the historian to state that it did not resolve those problems and in fact created new ones. Peace had been achieved but at what cost?

Further Reading

P. Birdsall, *Versailles Twenty Years After*, Archon, 1969, useful but prejudiced against Lloyd George.

R. B. Henig (ed.), *The League of Nations*, Oliver & Boyd, 1973, an excellent documentary study of the League with a good bibliography; the best starting point to this subject.

I. Lederer (ed.), *The Versailles Settlement. Was it Foredoomed to Failure?*, Heath, 1965, one of the 'Problems in European Civilization' series.

* A. J. Mayer, *Politics and Diplomacy of Peacemaking: containment and counterrevolution at Versailles, 1918–1919*, Weidenfeld & Nicolson, 1968, the essential basis for really serious work on this subject, but of formidable length.

H. Nicolson, *Peacemaking 1919*, Constable, 1933, a readable eye-witness account.

* H. W. V. Temperley (ed.), *History of the Peace Conference of Paris*, 6 volumes, Frowde and Hodder & Stoughton, 1920–4, the standard contemporary work of reference.

1 The Peace – an Ideal

. . . It is not too much to say that it [the war] has endangered the fabric of our civilization, and if it is to be repeated the whole European system may probably disappear in anarchy. It is surely, therefore, most urgent that we should try to think out some plan to lessen the possibility of future
5 war. . . .

What . . . can be done? The only possible way out appears to be to try to substitute for war some other way of settling international disputes. Two expedients suggest themselves: arbitration and conference of the Powers – European Concert. The difficulty of arbitration is to discover the arbitrators to whom sovereign powers will be content to submit questions of vital importance. The same objection does not apply to conferences. But, as we found in the present war, no machinery exists to force unwilling powers to agree to a conference and await its decision. It would be simple to include in the Treaty of Peace a general agreement to that effect. But what if a group of Powers were determined on war, how are they to be compelled to enter a conference? . . . I believe that in blockade as developed in this war such an instrument exists. . . .

> From a 'Memorandum on Proposals for Diminishing the Occasion of Future Wars', Autumn 1916, by Lord Robert Cecil, in R. B. Henig (ed.), *The League of Nations*, 1973, pp 21–4.

Questions

a What did Cecil mean by (i) 'the whole European system' (line 2); (ii) 'two expedients . . . European Concert' (lines 8–9); (iii) 'sovereign powers' (line 10); (iv) 'blockade' (line 17)?

b Who was Lord Robert Cecil and what role did he play in the international arena in the inter-war period?

c How did Cecil see future wars being avoided? Why were his suggestions not of major effect in the twenties and thirties?

* d Idealism was born out of the misery and horror that characterised the Great War. How far did the Treaty of Versailles live up to this idealism?

2 The Peace – a Word of Caution

There is a consideration in favour of a long-sighted peace which influences me even more than the desire to leave no causes justifying a fresh outbreak thirty years hence. There is one element in the present condition of nations which differentiates it from the situation as it was in 1815. In the Napoleonic war the countries were equally exhausted, but the revolutionary spirit had spent its force in the country of its birth, and Germany had satisfied legitimate popular demands for the time being by a series of economic changes which were inspired by courage, foresight and high statesmanship. The situation is very different now. The revolution is still in its infancy. The supreme figures of the Terror are still in command in Russia. The whole of Europe is filled with the spirit of revolution. There is everywhere a deep sense not only of discontent, but of anger and revolt amongst the workmen against pre-war conditions. The whole existing order in its political, social and economic aspects is questioned by the masses of the population from one end of Europe to the other. In some countries, like Germany and Russia, the unrest takes the form of open rebellion. . . . Much of this unrest is unhealthy. We shall never make a lasting peace by attempting to restore the conditions of 1914.

> From the Fontainebleau memorandum, 25 March 1919, in which Lloyd George warned against unreasonable peace conditions; in G. Schulz, *Revolutions and Peace Treaties 1917–1920*, p 225

Questions

a Explain the phrases (i) 'the Napoleonic war' (line 5); (ii) 'legitimate popular demands' (line 7); (iii) 'the Terror' (line 11).

b Who was Lloyd George and what role did he play during the war and as a peacemaker?

c The document contrasts the situation in 1815 with that in 1919. Explain these contrasts.

* *d* Lloyd George argued in the Fontainebleau memorandum for a peace which took the spirit of revolution into account (lines 11–12). How far did the final treaties achieve this?

3   Acceptance or Rejection — the Decision of Weimar

[Chancellor Gustav Bauer is speaking at this point in the debate] . . . 'Nevertheless to refuse would not be to avert. A "no" would be little more than the brief postponement of a "yes". We solemnly declare that we shall not sign this Treaty with conviction, but with the fullest mental
5   reservation. The mandate for our signature will, therefore, be worded as follows:

> The Government of the German Republic is ready to sign this Peace Treaty, but without implied admission in so doing that the German people were the first instigators of the war, and without engaging herself to comply with
10   Articles 227–230 [delivery of war criminals] of the Peace Treaty aforesaid.'

Paul Löbe spoke on behalf of the Social Democrats . . .
'Ladies and Gentlemen. — Our attitude as Social Democrats, as we face this great question, heavy with our fate, which to-day we are called upon to answer, is set down in the declaration I am to read to you.
15   'Germany's need weighs on us all. No matter how we may differ from one another in our attitude to this most horrible of wars, this most comfortless and desolate of Peace Treaties, we bear an equal weight in all our hearts. This National Assembly . . . is aware that we stand upon the threshold of the saddest years in German history. The Assembly may
20   decide to empower the new executive to decree the signing of these articles . . . but, that come what may — we will not sign it! But in either case we shall have begun a new age — an age of the direst want, of national poverty (Hear! Hear!). . . . Through the gates of this peace the German people must pass on, crushed with material poverty, spiritually

chained, morally oppressed — into the darkest time of care and suffering.

'The crime of this war is inexpiable; the bitterest remorse must harry whoever bears the guilt of having engendered it (Hear! Hear!). . . . Capitalism made this war. Imperialism made it. The peace they are forcing now upon the world is inflicting the deepest wounds on the German working class, on the working class in every country. To-day we have no alternative. No man can answer for calamities whose remedy is beyond his strength. All power to resist this peace has deserted us, and therefore we must shoulder and abide by it.

'. . . Our deputation did everything in its power to show the enemy that such a Treaty cannot be fulfilled. Our counter-proposals went to the limits of our capacity. . . . All to no purpose! . . . we demand that, once and for all, this ancient tradition of a lying diplomacy be broken, that our Government sign no formal obligation intending to put it aside as soon as appears expedient. Rather, for every people, even for Germany, let this new peace make one unshakeable law, lay down one sure foundation for a new community of nations. There must be no intention, either among our people or our rulers of secret or open violation. Enemy statesmen, in flagrant contradiction of such a principle, would force us to sign demands they themselves know can never be fulfilled. If we refuse, war will flame up again. Therefore we must decide which we intend — to sign this most drastic Treaty of conquest for a peace whose burden far exceeds our strength, or to expose our undefended land and countrymen to fresh cruelties and horrors of war. Were there any way of avoiding these fearful alternatives, no German would hesitate to take it. But there is no way.

'We cannot, we will not, recall our countrymen under arms. They are too enfeebled economically, too spiritually, too physically exhausted, to resist even for a month the preponderance of the victors' power. . . . We should drive to their deaths another hundred thousand men, our harvests would be destroyed, our country devastated, our economic life deprived of its last shreds of value. Food supplies from without would be cut off, our most essential railways would break down. . . . They would rob us of our last coal mines, bring all our industries to a standstill. . . . Within a very short time we should have to submit again, unconditionally, and sign an even bitterer peace. . . . And enemy Governments would use their despotic strength to stamp out every liberty the revolution has brought: they would dismember Germany and submit her to a permanent foreign yoke. The working class could be exploited to the uttermost and crushed, under a double burden of famine and pitiless forced labour. . . .

'Such Allied statesmen have always hated Germany, the original and future country of Socialism. This Capitalist, this Imperialist war closes with a Treaty designed to bar the way to Socialism against the whole German working class. . . . The world lies in wreckage about us. We want to help build it up anew in the spirit of amity among nations, on the basis of law and equality conformed to the eternal idea — Justice.'

Victor Schiff, *The Germans at Versailles 1919*, 1930, pp 150—5

. . . it was shown very clearly how hard it is to fight against the letter which defines 'rights' by treaty; how much formidable nationalist and militarist opposition still survives against the dictates of any policy of agreement and sane human understanding.

75 But what a change from then to now! These are negotiations, not mere dictates. Germany is no longer isolated; she has often been called upon to arbitrate between her conquerors of yesterday, her creditors of today. . . . The fantastic illusions, entertained ten years ago by our conquerors and set down in the Versailles Treaty, have long been utterly

80 dissipated. Present and future realities show more clearly than ever they did, from a financial standpoint even, the stupidity of modern war. . . .

> Victor Schiff, *op. cit.*, preface to the second German edition, pp 11—12

Questions

a (i) What is meant by the reservation 'without implied admission . . . the war' (lines 8—9) and why do you think the Germans maintained it?
(ii) What was 'This National Assembly' (line 18)?
(iii) What did Löbe mean when he spoke of the German people being 'crushed with material poverty, spiritually chained, morally oppressed' (lines 24—5)?
(iv) What is meant by 'unconditionally' (line 58) and 'the revolution' (line 60)?

b How effective a piece of oratory do you think Löbe's speech was? Would it have convinced you that signing the treaty was necessary?

c What did Löbe see as the cause of the war? Why did he hold such a view?

d What would be the consequences of (i) acceptance of the peace; (ii) rejection of the peace, according to Löbe?

* *e* Löbe saw the Treaty of Versailles as a triumph for conservatism over Socialism. How valid a conclusion is this?

* *f* For any peace to be lastingly successful both sides must accept it with conviction. Bauer's statement 'that we shall not sign this Treaty with conviction, but with the fullest mental reservation' meant that Versailles was not worth the paper it was written on. Discuss.

4 'The Stab in the Back' – German Militarism and Peace

The attitude of the officer corps towards the signing of the peace treaty was, as the Majority Socialists were forced to concede, a crucial factor in the Cabinet's deliberations. No group had more to lose by the terms of the peace treaty than the German armed forces. Moreover the officer corps

5 believed that it had been betrayed by the German government, which had made only the most cursory protests against the military clauses of the treaty. According to the reports which the Army received from its

representatives on the German delegation at Versailles, Brockdorff-Rantzau had given instructions to his staff that the Allies' military demands should go largely uncontested, in the hope that this could be bargained off against other objections. . . . In addition, the Supreme Command knew that the Foreign Minister himself was something of an anti-militarist. . . . Brockdorff-Rantzau had made quite clear his distrust of such figures as Ludendorff, as well as his conviction that the refusal of the officer corps to face reality and permit a negotiated peace was largely responsible for the position in which Germany now found herself.

Just before Brockdorff-Rantzau and his delegation left for Versailles, Groener had appeared before the full Cabinet in order to make clear the position of the Supreme Command. He urged that the maintenance of a large German Army based on universal conscription be made a cardinal objective of German diplomacy. Groener conceded that the Army had a somewhat reactionary reputation, but this, he said, was not the point. 'Only that government can govern which has military power . . . without power you can't rule. The Supreme Command takes the position that this is not a question of counterrevolution and reaction, but only of sound state power.'

. . . Brockdorff-Rantzau regarded Groener and his proposal with cold disdain. The spectacle of the Supreme Command again dictating foreign policy brought back unpleasant recollections. . . . Economic recovery and industrial strength were vastly more important objectives. He could not imagine a more unattractive (or less rewarding) prospect at Versailles than arguing in favour of a large German Army. . . .

This confrontation between the government and the Supreme Command came at a particularly unfortunate moment – a moment when a belief was beginning to sweep through the officer corps that it had been the victim of a Dolchstoss, a 'stab in the back', by certain faithless and cowardly citizens. Had it not been for this, the argument ran, the German Army would have won the war or, at the very least, would have fought the Allies to a standstill.

. . . The exact manner in which the Dolchstoss legend was born is unclear. One story, perhaps apocryphal, has it that Ludendorff dined with Sir Neill Malcolm, the head of the British military mission in Berlin. . . . In an unfortunate attempt to coalesce Ludendorff's rambling account [of the German revolutionaries], Malcolm suggested, 'Do you mean, General, that you were stabbed in the back?'

Ludendorff leaped at this. 'Yes, yes,' he cried, 'that's it exactly. We were stabbed in the back.'

From then on it became an article of faith among German officers that no less an authority than a British general had admitted that Germany had laid down her arms only when she had been betrayed at home. A neat web of supporting evidence was gathered to substantiate this claim. . . . Even Fritz Ebert, when welcoming the troops back to Berlin in December, had hailed them as returning 'unvanquished from the field'. . . . The Majority Socialists made little or no effort to counteract

the tale even though it should have been apparent to them that they would receive the lion's share of the blame. They chose to ignore the Dolchstoss charge — with the result that the officer corps was provided with a grievance which, when added to the provisions of the peace treaty,
60 was more than enough to convince the Army that it was the victim of treachery by the civil government.

. . . Germany agreed to reduce her Navy to a shadow of its prewar glory. The Army was a different matter.

. . . the Allies had no doubt that within a decade, or at most two
65 decades, Germany could rebuild her Army into what it had been before. . . . The backbone of the old Imperial Army, the officer corps, was still very much in existence and was prepared — indeed, anxious — to supply the leadership for a reborn Army of awesome size.

The Allies had no intention of permitting this to occur. . . . The Allies
70 had suffered far too much at the hands of the German Army, and had come too close to losing the war, to consider any appeal on behalf of German militarism. The only real questions at Versailles regarding the German military were how small an army Germany should be permitted and how it should be recruited — and those were matters that the Allies
75 debated among themselves. The attitude of the officer corps towards the peace treaty was no secret to the civil government and was the source of great apprehension. . . . The only possibility for a successful defence [in case of an Allied invasion] was a levee en masse. If the people were willing to sell their lives, to accept the destruction of their cities and to endure the
80 most catastrophic sacrifices, the country might possibly be defended. . . .

Groener had only this realistic reply: 'The significance of such a gesture would escape the German people. There would be a general outcry against counter revolution and militarism. The result would be the downfall of the Reich. The Allies . . . would show themselves pitiless.
85 The officer corps would be destroyed and the name of Germany would disappear from the map.'

R. Watt, *The Kings Depart — The Tragedy of Germany: Versailles and the German Revolution*, 1969, pp 462–7, 475–6

Questions

a (i) Who were the following people and what part did they play in the post-war peace: Brockdorff-Rantzau (lines 8–9), Luden-dorff (line 14), Groener (line 19)?

(ii) Explain the meaning of 'The Majority Socialists' (line 2); 'based on universal conscription' (line 21); 'a Dolchstoss' (line 41); 'a levee en masse' (line 78).

(iii) 'In addition . . . an anti-militarist' (lines 11–13). Explain this passage and show why this situation was a cause of conflict.

(iv) In what ways had 'Germany agreed to reduce her Navy to a shadow of its prewar glory' (lines 62–3)?

(v) How had the Allies 'come too close to losing the war' (line 71)?

<blockquote>
b In what ways does this passage show the major differences between the German Supreme Command and the Cabinet in the immediate post-war period? Were these problems ever to be resolved?

c Why did the civil government adopt an anti-militarist position at Versailles?

d The idea of a 'stab in the back' as the cause of Germany's defeat in 1918 shows the importance of the myth in history. Discuss.

* <i>e</i> For the German army, particularly the officer corps, Versailles was peace without honour. How important was this in the history of Germany to 1933?
</blockquote>

5 Versailles – Raison d'être and Revision

. . . Ideally real peace presupposes a full understanding of the true causes of a war; it demands the complete removal of these causes and the replacement of old political and economic structures by new ones which have none of the qualities known to cause wars. No doubt this is a
5   Utopian principle, a truth that has not become reality anywhere. But it should be voiced if only to highlight the difficulty of judging peace treaties and to point out the magnitude of the task of peacemaking – if the establishment of peace is to mean something more than the end of war. . . . Emphasis has rightly been put on the basic difference between
10 past peace treaties which frequently contained some special clause explicitly providing for what Fritz Dickman has called the 'forgetting that helps to establish peace', and the discriminatory settlements of recent times. . . .

In the First World War the differences between people and ideas
15 rapidly became extreme. By 1917 the Allies were convinced that they were fighting for a democratic world against antiquated monarchical autocracies. But from the start it was assumed that German policy was to blame for the war and that the Kaiser must be held responsible. Clemenceau and Lloyd George and also Wilson thought so. But in the
20 conclusions they drew from this they were agreed only in the need to overthrow the Kaiser. They differed profoundly in their approach to the practical and legal implications of Germany's assumed guilt and to the peace treaty.

The concrete problems that presented themselves to the peacemakers
25 at the end of the First World War arose from the discrepancy between Wilson's material proposals and above all the spiritual content of his peace messages and the irreparable situation created by the war. The peace which Wilson wanted, his 'new order of things', was to be a peace of justice and of clear conscience; it would end the age of imperialism and
30 create a new world under the auspices of the 'Covenant League of Nations'. . . . The war had ended with the collapse of the strongest military powers in Europe; they could therefore not make any significant contribution to the discussion on the shape of the future peace. For the

moment the Allies were therefore objectively free to decide their policies
35 without limiting factors. . . .

The peacemakers failed to establish a permanent order. Their work
continued the political transformation of the world begun with the war;
but they did not find the lasting state of calm for which humanity longed
after experiencing to the full the horrors of war and after making
40 such terrible sacrifices. The great movements of the age did not come to
a stop.

If one examines the work of the Paris conference one finds errors and
mistakes in rich measure and can criticise to one's heart's content. The
Swiss historian Leonhard von Muralt described the 'System of Versailles'
45 as the result of 'wrong power politics', power politics that failed to 'take
all relevant issues into consideration'. But what in 1919 were 'all relevant
issues'? . . .

It is understandable that in Germany in the conditions prevailing in the
post-war period the peace treaty was condemned as the 'dictated peace of
50 Versailles' and was judged in the light of Germany's territorial losses and
military, financial and economic burdens; but this does not do justice to
the real state of affairs. . . . The fundamental problem which is also at the
heart of the more penetrating subsequent criticism of the 'System of
Versailles' continued to exist after the conclusion of peace. This was the
55 problem of establishing a sound political equilibrium in Europe not based
merely on the distribution of power as it was at the end of the war. Yet
how could a new balance of power be achieved while the Western
powers were fighting Russia or trying to isolate it and while Russia was
threatening to expand westwards? How could there be an equilibrium
60 when a number of new states were emerging at the European periphery
of old Russia and others resulting from the break-up of the Danube
monarchy, and when their internal situation, their reactions in the
international sphere and their economic potential were totally unknown
quantities? How could there be equilibrium if it was impossible for
65 statesmen accurately to take into account the invisible forces of both great
and small states that had been irresistibly mobilised by the war? How
could there be a lasting settlement that took account of all the elements
that would be of importance in a radically changed world? There is a
serious lack of logic in all verdicts passed on the peace treaty which ignore
70 the fact that the pre-war policies could not prevent war and which fail to
appreciate the essential continuity of the pre-war period, the war, peace-
time and the era of revision.

. . . The historian only does justice to his legitimate task if he detaches
himself from contemporary judgments with their overdependence on
75 first impressions. There is a wide gap between the real significance of the
peace treaties and the subjective verdict passed on them. Yet both were
undoubtedly of great political importance. . . .

. . . the war time friend-enemy approach lived on in the minds of
many people. Reference was made to the 'enemy' after 1918 in almost
80 the same tone as during the war. This was primarily due to the continued

existence of nationalism. But it was also the result of the political conditions in Europe where the new order was based on friend-enemy relations which were broken down only slowly and reluctantly and which were by no means overcome by the early efforts of the League of
85 Nations. The prolonged effects as well as the complexity of the consequences of the peace treaties created new tensions and conflicts and gave new food to deeply rooted national differences. . . .

The German protest against Versailles never ceased and in Germany the revision of the peace treaty seemed of greater importance than all else.
90 Versailles cast its shadow over German policy at home and abroad and with the force of a compulsive idea this policy was guided into the channels of nationalistic reaction. . . . Simultaneously two legends were born and before the year 1919 was out they began to confuse the issues: the Wilson legend which claimed that from the outset Wilson had been
95 determined to join the war, a claim that was said to be confirmed by the peace of Versailles which no longer had anything in common with a peace of the Fourteen Points; and the 'stab in the back' legend according to which the German army would have been victorious had it not been 'stabbed in the back' by revolt at home. It was not the army that had
100 failed; the Army High Command had acted correctly. The collapse was entirely the fault of the 'German revolution'. . . . In fact the 'system of Versailles' failed not because the treaties were worthless, not because mistakes were made, but primarily because there was no timely or far-sighted attempt to revise these treaties and to continue the necessarily
105 unfinished work of the Paris Peace Conference. As it was the criteria established were obstinately adhered to even when the belief in their usefulness and viability had begun to vanish.

G. Schulz, *Revolutions and Peace Treaties 1917–1920*, 1972, pp 135–7, 143, 222–4, 226–9, 236

Questions

a (i) What is the meaning of the following: 'a Utopian principle' (line 5); 'the Kaiser' (line 18); 'the spiritual content of his peace messages' (lines 26–7); 'dictated peace of Versailles' (lines 49–50); 'the Danube monarchy' (lines 61–2); 'the continued existence of nationalism' (lines 80–1) and 'the Fourteen Points' (line 97)?

(ii) What do you think Dickman means by 'forgetting that helps to establish peace' (lines 11–12)?

(iii) Were the allies 'fighting for a democratic world against antiquated monarchical autocracies' (lines 16–17)?

(iv) Why could the defeated powers not 'make any significant contribution . . . future peace' (lines 32–3)?

(v) Explain the reference to Russia in lines 57–9.

b What does Schulz see as the prerequisite for a real peace? Why was Versailles not a real peace?

* *c* What do you think were 'all relevant issues' in 1919 that the

peacemakers needed to take into account (lines 45–6)? Which did they fail to take into account?

d   Why could sound political equilibrium not be established in 1919?

* e   To Germany revision of the Versailles settlement was fundamental. Why was it never achieved?

* f   Schultz argues that there is a wide gap between 'the real significance of the peace treaties and the subjective verdict passed on them'. Explain the importance of this distinction in the light of the next twenty years.

Further Work

a   How far did the personalities of Wilson, Lloyd George and Clemenceau play a dominant role in Paris in 1919?

b   The chapter has concentrated on the failure of Versailles to satisfy either the ideals or the practical problems of a lasting peace. Examine how far the other peace treaties also failed to resolve these problems.

c   Examine the development of the League of Nations in the inter-war period. Could it have prevented war in 1939? Why did it fail to do so?

d   'Russia played a more vital part at Paris than Prussia. For the Prussian idea had been utterly defeated, while the Russian idea was still rising in power.' Was the containment of Bolshevism the over-riding objective of the Versailles settlement?

* e   With the advantage of hindsight the historian can see the basic flaws of the Versailles settlement. Why did the participants in the conference fail to see them?

II   The Weimar Republic

Introduction

D. C. Watt wrote that in the Europe after the First World War, 'what was at issue was the collapse of the hitherto accepted basis of authority and legitimacy and the failure to find any alternative to them. The process can be seen at its strongest in Germany, where the revolution of 1918 and the abdication of the Kaiser initiated a period in which the legitimacy of the Republic of Weimar was challenged both by left and right. . . .'

The Weimar Republic is almost inevitably over-shadowed by the Third Reich, and the danger exists of seeing the Republic as no more than an aberration in the 'traditional authoritarian' governments of Prussia/Germany; in this view the Republic was doomed from birth. Perhaps the apparent success of the Bundesrepublik in West Germany today should tempt the historian away from the fallacy of *post hoc, ergo propter hoc.*

Why the Republic failed, which is also a feature of section VII, and the interplay of events and personalities deserve serious consideration, especially the impact of the First World War and the peace treaties, the growth of extremism, and the role of the Reichswehr.

The leading Weimar politicians require close scrutiny, especially Stresemann, Bruning and Hindenburg. To what extent was Stresemann a success in domestic and foreign policies? What were the rôles of Brüning and Hindenburg in the Republic's demise?

In the style of the American historian Fogel, it might be worthwhile to attempt counter-factual analysis: could the Republic have survived if the allies had shown greater leniency over reparations in the 1920s? If Stresemann had lived beyond 1929 . . .? If the president had been more favourable to Weimar . . .? The documents offer a guide to many of these questions, and the key to many of the answers lies in the débâcle of 1918. In the long term, an understanding of the history of Germany must rest on more fundamental inquiries.

Further Reading

F. L. Carsten, *The Reichswehr and Politics, 1918 to 1933,* Oxford University Press, 1966, and G. A. Craig, *The Politics of the Prussian Army 1640–1945,* Oxford University Press, 1955; two important books on the significant part played by the army in the Republic.

P. Gay, *Weimar Culture: the outsider as insider*, Secker & Warburg, 1969, a readable study of aspects of Weimar and Nazi culture.

J. W. Hiden, *The Weimar Republic*, Longman, 1974, a good documentary collection with sound introductory chapters.

G. Mann, *The History of Germany since 1789*, Chatto & Windus, 1968, the stimulating study by Thomas Mann's son, in translation.

A. J. Nicholls, *Weimar and the Rise of Hitler*, Macmillan, 1968, a very useful introduction for sixth formers.

1 The Problems

The root causes of the German question were — very broadly speaking — retarded unification (and therefore nationhood), capitalism maturing in a late-feudal setting, and a national preference for *konflictlose* synthesis (synthesis without conflict).

5   Germany's belated emergence as a great power, which led her to a preoccupation with foreign policy and a neglect of home policy and reforms, marked and distorted all her subsequent development. This distortion was compounded by another. In 1871 industry had brought German military triumph, statehood and great-power status, but the

10   agents of that victory — the middle classes — failed to gain their own political victory, or even a commensurate share of power. . . .

Foreign policy ceased to be Germany's main concern when she became an object rather than a subject in world affairs. The collapse of the Empire put an end to pseudo-constitutionalism and to the exclusion of com-

15   moners from political power. The chimera of *konfliktlosigkeit* faded further as the Weimar Republic articulated — and tried to institutionalize — the interplay of contending social and political forces.

One of the most poignant aspects of 1918 – 19 was that it was the first, and therefore the seminal, instance in Germany of alternating political

20   parties in office — the essence of the democratic process. The Social Democrats, Left Liberals and Catholic Centre, which under the Empire had been permanently relegated to the opposition benches, now became the government — but their assumption of office owed less, in the last analysis, to the ballot-box (and to the barricades put up in November

25   1918) than to Allied arms.

In 1918 – 19 most Germans became democrats. Even the 'national classes' took up democracy — as a means of obtaining easier peace terms from the West and of fending off Bolshevism in the East. Versailles and the failure of revolution to take root outside Russia soon ended their

30   aberration; democracy once again became an alien device, a creed whose victory had resulted from German defeat, and bitterness at losing the war threw into lurid relief the gain of power by an inexperienced minority.

Weimar's office-holders were indeed a new, and — thanks to the Imperial constitution — a somewhat *parvenu* élite. The Social Democrat,

35   Ebert, who replaced the Kaiser as head of state was a master-sadler.

Similarly suspect (in Conservative eyes) were figures whom the November 1918 upheaval had catapulted into the centre of the political stage: journalists such as Theodor Wolff, editor of the *Berliner Tageblatt* and co-founder of the *Demokratische Partei*, as well as Leftist writers such as Ernst Toller, a participant of the short-lived Bavarian Soviet Republic of 1919. Politically Toller was at the opposite end of the left-wing spectrum to Ebert, who – 'hating social revolution like sin' – approved of the suppression of the Munich Soviet, though the Right persisted in lumping together Social Democrats and revolutionary socialists as Marxist scum. . . .

A climate envenomed by character assassination bred physical assassins. Rosa Luxemburg was murdered by officers 'collaborating' with the Ebert government, and *Fehme* gunmen killed the Catholic Centre leader Erzberger who had signed the Versailles Treaty, and the 'Judeo-Democrat' Foreign Minister Rathenau who strove to implement it. The courts treated right-wing terrorism with a leniency best exemplified by Hitler's one year jail term after the bloodily abortive Munich putsch of November 1923. The whole tenor of political court decisions high-lighted a crucial flaw of the new state: though its law-making was democratic the application of the law had remained in the hands of anti-democrats.

The death of the Republic which this division foreshadowed – and ultimately precipitated – occurred in two stages. While the majority of the people actively deserted democracy only during the Depression, the majority of the élite (the civil service, the judiciary, the officer corps, the academics and even the clergy) had rejected it virtually at birth. . . .

The Jews became the embodiment, on a scale unprecedented in history, of every ill besetting state and society in the final stage of the Weimar Republic. A few prominent Jews had helped to found the Republic, or been active in the Press, in literature and the theatre – the arenas in which battle had been joined between order and freedom, between archaic and permissive attitudes. Jews had espoused internationalism – the majority as partisans of the League of Nations and a few as Marxists or pacifists. Some of them were practitioners of psychoanalysis, others pioneered new ways of tackling problems such as abortion, homosexuality, criminology or penology.

If the relaxation of censorship in the Weimar era led to the publication of lesbian and homosexual magazines, and discussion and literature on all aspects of sex and the human psyche proliferated; if there was an economically conditioned increase in the incidence of abortion and the number of juvenile prostitutes (male as well as female); if some advanced schools included sex-education in their curriculum and had pupil committees claiming shop-steward status, it was tempting to echo Treitschke's phrase 'The Jews are our misfortune'. The Judeo-democracy was blamed for the twenties cult of the new, the meretricious and the sensational that saddled Germany with twice its pre-war cosmetics bill, fostered the smoking habit among women, riveted public attention on

six-day bicycle races, and pruriently reported murder trials. Yet the main
charge against the Jews was that they dominated such spheres as banking,
85 business, real estate, brokerage, moneylending and cattle trading.

> R. Grunberger, *A Social History of the Third Reich*, 1971, pp 1 – 3,
> 15 – 16

Questions

a   Define 'capitalism maturing in a late-feudal setting' (lines 2 – 3);
'synthesis without conflict' (line 4); 'seminal' (line 19); '*parvenu*' (line
34); 'penology' (line 71); 'pruriently' (line 83).

b   What does the author see as Germany's problems before 1918?
Examine each with reference to the problems of the Weimar
Republic.

c   Why was democracy linked with defeat?

*   d   What reasons underlay the rejection of the Republic by the élite (lines
60 – 1)?

e   Why did Jews become an object of hatred in Weimar Germany?

*   f   What aspects of imperial Germany were retained by the new
Republic? Assess the reasons for their retention, and their importance.

2   The Army

In the years that followed the Kapp *Putsch*, the German army was
transformed from an aggregation of disparate and ill co-ordinated units
with a resentful and demoralized officer corps into a homogeneous and
perfectly disciplined force which, in quality at least, had no equal in
5   Europe. By an adroit combination of passive resistance to, and skilful
evasion of, the restrictive clauses of the Versailles Treaty, it advanced
much further along the road of military recovery than had been thought
remotely possible by the men who had drafted those clauses in 1919; and,
before the end of the decade, it had laid the foundations for its later
10 expansion under Hitler.

In the same years, while ostentatiously abstaining from politics, the
army steadily increased its influence in every aspect of state affairs and did
not hesitate, on occasion, to arrogate to itself the initiative in matters of
policy formulation, especially in the foreign sphere. This development,
15 not unnaturally, caused concern in parliamentary circles, notably among
the parties of the left, who were, nevertheless, powerless to control it. . . .

. . . the chief of the army command was determined that the
Reichswehr must make up in overall efficiency for what it must lose
because of its limited size. He demonstrated this by the attention which
20 he paid to matters of selection and training, the eagerness with
which he grasped at the latest technical innovations, and the emphasis
which he placed upon tactical and strategical improvements as he
proceeded with his work.

The very necessity of reducing the army so sharply enabled Seeckt to start with an *élite* force. With respect to the officer corps, for instance, he was forced to dismiss three out of every four active officers; and, quite logically, he saw to it that it was the most intelligent officers and those who had proved themselves to be the most courageous and most reliable leaders of troops who were retained. In subsequent years, as new openings appeared in the officer corps, the most stringent requirements were laid down for aspirants to commissions. . . . Seeckt's personal preference was always for candidates who were of aristocratic birth and descended from the old military families, for he believed in carrying the tradition of the old army over into the new; but he never permitted this bias to protect officers from the rigorous educational and training requirements which he had laid down. . . .

In the rigorous training programme which he enforced upon all ranks, Seeckt placed special emphasis upon technical and weapons training, co-ordination of arms, an effective system of communications, and a continued devotion to the Prussian tradition of mobility. The Versailles Treaty had, of course, placed difficult obstacles in his way by denying Germany the use of offensive weapons – including military aircraft, armour, and heavy artillery. But much could be accomplished within treaty limits. Every officer and man was trained in the expert use of small arms and machine guns and in methods of communication in the field; and officers were sent to the Berlin *Technische Hochschule* in order that the latest technical advances might be studied for possible military application. Studies of co-ordination and communication were encouraged and tested in elaborate exercises. Manoeuvres with motorized units were held in the Harz mountains as early as 1921; and in the winter of 1923 – 4 Lieutenant-Colonel von Brauchitsch, who was later to be commander-in-chief of the army, organized manoeuvres to test the possibilites of employing motorized troops in co-operation with aircraft. . . .

Seeckt . . . from the very beginning of his term in the *Heeresleitung*, emphasized the superiority of offensive to defensive strategy and based his whole training programme on the assumption that it was strategical mobility that won wars. Despite the fact that the Reichswehr would, in his opinion, probably be inferior in numbers and material to the armies of neighbouring powers for a long time to come, Seeckt held to the traditional Prussian view that 'destruction of the opposing army . . . is still the highest law of war, although at times it may assume a different appearance'; and he impressed upon his officers the idea that 'the goal of a modern strategy will be to force a decision with forces which are mobile and highly developed in operational capacity . . . before the masses have begun to move'. Here, in germ at least, was the idea of the *attaque brusquée* or lightning war which was to become dogma in the German army.

Even within the limitations of the treaty, then, Seeckt was able to accomplish a good deal for the new Reichswehr. But he was not content to stop there. From the beginning, his public programme of reconstruction was supplemented with important secret practices and policies which were designed to evade and circumvent the stipulations of Versailles.

G. A. Craig, *The Politics of the Prussian Army, 1640–1945*, 1955, pp 382, 393–7

Questions

a Identify 'Kapp *Putsch*' (line 1); 'Seeckt' (line 24); '*Heeresleitung*' (line 55).

b What measures were taken to improve the officer corps in the 1920s? Why were these measures important?

c Examine the contribution of the early motorised manoeuvres to the success of Germany to 1942.

d What was von Seeckt's importance to (i) 'the 100,000-Man Reichswehr' and (ii) the Weimar Republic?

* e In what ways were the military clauses of Versailles circumvented?

* f What is implicit in the use of 'Prussian' to describe the German army from 1871? Briefly examine the rôle of the army in Prussia/Germany from the mid-seventeenth century.

g Golo Mann wrote 'that which could never integrate itself, with the best will in the world could not integrate the army'. How valid is this viewpoint?

3 Elections

Weimar election results

Totals on register (in mills.)	19 Jan 1919	6 June 1920	4 May 1924	7 Dec 1924	20 May 1928	14 Sep 1930	31 July 1932	6 Nov 1932
	36.8	35.9	38.4	39.0	41.2	43.0	44.2	44.4
Percentage of voters	82.7	79.1	77.4	78.8	75.6	82.0	84.0	80.6
NSDAP								
Seats	—	—	32	14	12	107	230	196
Per cent	—	—	6.6	3.0	2.6	18.3	37.4	33.1
DNVP								
Seats	44	71	95	103	73	41	37	52
Per cent	10.3	15.1	19.5	20.5	14.2	7.0	5.9	8.8
DVP								
Seats	19	65	45	51	45	30	7	11
Per cent	4.4	14.0	9.2	10.1	8.7	4.5	1.2	1.9
Centre & BVP								
Seats	91	85	81	88	78	87	98	90
Per cent	19.7	17.9	15.6	17.3	15.1	14.8	15.9	15.0
DDP								
Seats	75	39	28	32	25	20	4	2
Per cent	18.6	8.3	5.7	6.3	3.8	3.6	1.0	1.0

Weimar election results (*contd*)

SPD								
Seats	165	102	100	131	153	143	133	121
Per cent	37.9	21.6	20.5	26.0	29.8	24.5	21.6	20.4

USPD								
Seats	22	84						
Per cent	7.8	17.9	0.8					

KPD								
Seats	—	4	62	45	54	77	89	100
Per cent	—	2.1	12.6	9.0	10.6	14.3	14.6	16.9

Number of deputies in the Reichstag	421	459	472	493	491	577	608	584
Votes cast in millions	30.4	28.2	29.3	30.3	30.8	35.0	36.9	35.5

[The political allegiance of the parties is on a vertical plane, from extreme right-wing at the top to extreme left-wing at the bottom.]

G. Castellan, *L'Allemagne de Weimar 1918–1933*, Paris, 1969, p 117, quoted in J. W. Hiden, *The Weimar Republic*, 1974, p 81

Questions

a Identify the political parties mentioned.

* *b* Which of the parties had existed in imperial Germany?

c Which parties during this period (i) lost seats, (ii) gained seats, (iii) remained virtually stable?

d Who lost votes to the Nazis? Why may this have taken place?

e What information on the electoral success of the NSDAP is concealed by these statistics?

* *f* What electoral system did the Weimar Republic have? How did it affect the crises afflicting the Republic from 1929 to 1933?

4 Weimar Twilight

Like a long train which stops at every dingy little station, the winter dragged slowly past. Each week there were new emergency decrees. Brüning's weary episcopal voice issued commands to the shopkeepers, and was not obeyed. 'It's Fascism,' complained the Social Democrats. 'He's weak,' said Helen Pratt. 'What these swine need is a man with hair on his chest.'. . . People said that the Nazis would be in power by Christmas; but Christmas came and they were not. . . .

Berlin was in a state of civil war. Hate exploded suddenly, without warning, out of nowhere; at street corners, in restaurants, cinemas, dance halls, swimming-baths; at midnight, after breakfast, in the middle of the afternoon. Knives were whipped out, blows were dealt with spiked rings, beer-mugs, chair-legs, or leaded clubs; bullets slashed the advertisements on the poster-columns, rebounded from the iron roofs of latrines. In the

middle of a crowded street a young man would be attacked, stripped,
15 thrashed, and left bleeding on the pavement; in fifteen seconds it was all
over and the assailants had disappeared. Otto got a gash over the eye with
a razor in a battle on a fair-ground near the Copernickerstrasse. The
doctor put in three stitches and he was in hospital for a week. The
newspapers were full of death-bed photographs of rival martyrs, Nazi,
20 Reichsbanner, and Communist. My pupils looked at them and shook
their heads, apologizing to me for the state of Germany. 'Dear, dear!' they
said, 'it's terrible. It can't go on.'

The murder reporters and the jazz-writers had inflated the German
language beyond recall. The vocabulary of newspaper invective (traitor,
25 Versailles-lackey, murder-swine, Marx-crook, Hitler-swamp, Red-pest)
had come to resemble, through excessive use, the formal phraseology of
politeness employed by the Chinese. The word *Liebe*, soaring from the
Goethe standard, was no longer worth a whore's kiss. *Spring, moonlight,
youth, roses, girl, darlings, heart, May*: such were the miserably devaluated
30 currency dealt in by the authors of all those tangoes, waltzes, and fox-
trots which advocated the private escape. Find a dear little sweetheart,
they advised, and forget the slump, ignore the unemployed. Fly, they
urged us, to Hawaii, to Naples, to the Never-Never-Vienna.
Hugenberg . . . was serving up nationalism to suit all tastes. He
35 produced battlefield epics, farces of barrack-room life, operettas in which
the jinks of a pre-war military aristocracy were reclothed in the fashions
of 1932. His brilliant directors and cameramen had to concentrate their
talents on cynically beautiful shots of the bubbles in champagne and the
sheen of lamplight on silk.

40 And morning after morning, all over the immense, damp, dreary town
and the packing-case colonies of huts in the suburb allotments, young
men were waking up to another workless empty day to be spent as they
could best contrive; selling boot-laces, begging, playing draughts in the
hall of the Labour Exchange, hanging about urinals, opening the doors of
45 cars, helping with crates in the markets, gossiping, lounging, stealing,
overhearing racing tips, sharing stumps of cigarette-ends picked up in the
gutter, singing folk-songs for groschen in courtyards and between
stations in the carriages of the Underground Railway. After the New
Year, the snow fell, but did not lie; there was no money to be earned by
50 sweeping it away. The shopkeepers rang all the coins on the counter for
fear of the forgers. Frl. Schroeder's astrologer foretold the end of the
world. 'Listen,' said Fritz Wendel, between sips of a cocktail in the bar of
the Eden Hotel, 'I give a damn if this country goes communist. What I
mean, we'd have to alter our ideas a bit. Hell, who cares?'

55 At the beginning of March, the posters for the Presidential Election
began to appear. Hindenburg's portrait, with an inscription in gothic
lettering beneath it, struck a frankly religious note: 'He hath kept faith
with you; be ye faithful unto Him.' The Nazis managed to evolve a
formula which dealt cleverly with this venerable icon and avoided the
60 offence of blasphemy: 'Honour Hindenburg; Vote for Hitler.' Otto and

his comrades set out every night, with paint-pots and brushes, on dangerous expeditions. They climbed high walls, scrambled along roofs, squirmed under hoardings; avoiding the police and the S.A. patrols. And next morning, passers-by would see Thälmann's name boldly inscribed in some prominent and inaccessible position. Otto gave me a bunch of little gum-backed labels: Vote for Thälmann, the Workers' Candidate. I carried these about in my pocket and stuck them on shop windows and doors when nobody was looking.

Brüning spoke in the Sport Palace. We must vote for Hindenburg, he told us, and save Germany. His gestures were sharp and admonitory; his spectacles gleamed emotion in the limelight. His voice quivered with dry academic passion. 'Inflation,' he threatened, and the audience shuddered. 'Tannenberg,' he reverently reminded: there was prolonged applause.

Bayer spoke in the Lustgarten, during a snowstorm, from the roof of a van; a tiny, hatless figure gesticulating above the vast heaving sea of faces and banners. Behind him was the cold facade of the Schloss; and, lining its stone balustrade, the ranks of armed silent police. 'Look at them,' cried Bayer. 'Poor chaps! it seems a shame to make them stand out of doors in weather like this. Never mind; they've got nice thick coats to keep them warm. Who gave them those coats? We did. Wasn't it kind of us? And who's going to give *us* coats? Ask me another.'

C. Isherwood, *Mr Norris Changes Trains*, 1935, Penguin edn 1942, pp 88—91

Questions

a In which year did the events described by Isherwood take place? What evidence suggests this?

b Which aspects of Berlin at this time favoured the growth of extremist parties?

c Why did the words 'Inflation' and 'Tannenberg' have such an effect on Brüning's audience (lines 72—3)?

d Has fiction any value for the historian? How reliable is Isherwood likely to be as an eye-witness?

* *e* 'A Zero paving the way for Nero.' (T. Lessing) Assess the impact of Hindenburg as president of the republic from 1925.

* *f* 'Under the double stress of its economic and its political trouble, the Reich in the early 1930's seemed to be on the point of disintegration or total collapse.' (G. A. Craig) Discuss this statement in the light of the extracts in this section.

Further Work

a Sir Edward Grey wrote in 1914 that 'the lees left by Bismarck still foul the cup'. To what extent was this true of Germany in the period of the Weimar Republic?

b Assess the validity of the following statements in view of the rôle of army leaders from 1918 to 1933.

'. . . there is no period in German history in which representatives of the army intervened more frequently and more directly in the internal politics of the country; but, it must be added, there is no period in which the results of this intervention were more unfortunate.' (G. A. Craig)

'. . . the policy of the army command . . . led to a weakening of the republic and of the organizations willing to defend it.' (F. L. Carsten)

c 'Reparations counted as a symbol. They created resentment, suspicion, and international hostility. More than anything else, they cleared the way for the second World war.' (A. J. P. Taylor) Trace the history of reparations during the period of the Weimar Republic.

III Russia and Revolution –
A Question of Causation

Introduction

One of the major problems which the historian has to face is that of causation, or why a particular event or series of events occurred. This problem becomes more difficult the more recent the events. The situation is aggravated on almost every major issue in Soviet history since there is not only widespread disagreement between Communist and non-Communist writers, but between Communists writing at different periods. It is not our intention to consider the Russian Revolution from varying historiographical viewpoints, though this is certainly one valid approach to the issue, but by posing the question 'did the 1914–17 war accentuate the collapse of the Tsarist system?'

E. H. Carr in his *What is History?* provides a useful view of causation which, given his own work on the Russian Revolution, has a particular significance. He argues that

> The historian deals in a multiplicity of causes. If he were required to consider the causes of the Bolshevik Revolution, he might name Russia's successive military defeats, the collapse of the Russian economy under the pressure of war, the effective propaganda of the Bolsheviks . . . in short, a random jumble of economic, political, ideological and personal causes, of long-term and short-term causes.

and that

> The true historian, confronted with this list of causes of his own compiling, would feel a professional compulsion to reduce it to order, to establish some hierarchy of causes which would fix their relation to one another, perhaps, to decide which cause or category of causes, should be regarded . . . the cause of all causes.

The historian is compelled to order the past to make it understandable for the present. This means identifying causes of events. Was the war the 'cause of all causes?'

The documents below attempt to place the revolutions of 1917 within the framework of economic and moral decay that characterised Russia in the first two decades of the twentieth century. The conversation between Ganz and an anonymous Russian official clearly shows a lack of morale and a pessimistic sense of the coming deluge. In fact the outbreak of war in 1914 saw this feeling of foreboding stemmed through an expression of intense patriotic fervour, the illogicality of which Solzhenitsyn shows in literary form. Both these documents raise important methodological problems for the historian. The question of their reliability and value is of utmost importance.

The military defeats of 1914 and 1915 at Tannenberg and the Masurian Lakes cracked wide open the facade of patriotism. Russia's total failure to cope with modern warfare is made clear in the police report of 1916 by which time the food shortages, the terrible loss of life and confidence and a resurgence of disgust for autocracy had once again brought Russia to the brink of revolutionary change. The chaos of 1917 when 'power fell into the streets' was capitalised upon by the Germans who allowed Lenin to return in the 'sealed train' to the Finland Station. The reasons for this are outlined in the German memoranda of March–April 1917 and in the modern account by Adam Ulam. Lenin symbolised both the chaos of revolution and the stability of the post-revolutionary settlement. As Florinsky makes clear, Lenin was the captain Tsarist Russia did not possess, even if the Bolsheviks were the skilled and highly disciplined crew. He alone had the pragmatism to take advantage of the confusion, indecision and fear, and successfully to forge the new Soviet state.

Further Reading

E. H. Carr, *The Bolshevik Revolution 1917–23*, 3 volumes, Macmillan, 1950–3, the definitive study in English.

Edward Crankshaw, *The Shadow of the Winter Palace—the drift to revolution 1825–1917*, Macmillan, 1976, a very readable, comprehensive and provocative history of the century before the Revolution.

Lionel Kochan, *The Making of Modern Russia*, Penguin, 1966, a good general history of the pre-revolutionary and Soviet periods.

Lionel Kochan, *Russia in Revolution 1890–1918*, Penguin, 1973.

J. P. Nettl, *The Soviet Achievement*, Thames and Hudson, 1969, a good, well-illustrated book which in its opening chapters deals with the pre-revolutionary situation.

Alec Nove, *An Economic History of the U.S.S.R.*, Penguin, 1976, a good starting point on the vexed question of Russian economic development.

* Hugh Seton-Watson, *The Russian Empire 1801–1917*, Oxford University Press, 1967, a compendious study.

1 Forebodings of Economic Doom

'What will be the end, then?'

'The end will be that the terror from above will awaken the terror from below, that peasant revolts will break out and assassinations will increase.'

5 'And is there no possibility of organizing the revolution so that it will not rage senselessly?'

'Impossible. . . .'

'There is no one with whom I have spoken who would fail to paint the future of this country in the darkest terms. Can there be no change of the fatal policy which is ruining the country?'

'Not before a great general catastrophe. When we shall be compelled for the first time partly to repudiate our debts — and that may happen sooner than we now believe — on that day, being no longer able to conceal our internal bankruptcy from foreign countries and from the Emperor — steps will be taken, perhaps. . . .'

'Is there no mistake possible here in what you are saying?'

'Whoever, like myself, has known the state kitchen for the last twenty-five years has no longer any doubts. The autocracy is not equal to the problems of a modern great power, and it would be against all historical precedent to assume that it would voluntarily yield without external pressure to a constitutional form of government.'

'We must wish then, for Russia's sake, that the catastrophe comes as quickly as possible.'

'I repeat to you that it is perhaps nearer than we all think or are willing to admit. That is the hope; that is our secret consolation. . . . We are near to collapse, like an athlete with great muscles and perhaps incurable heart weakness. We still maintain ourselves upright by stimulants, by loans, which like all stimulants only help to ruin the system more quickly. With that we are a rich country with all conceivable resources, simply ill-governed and prevented from unlocking our resources. But is this the first time that quacks have ruined a Hercules that has fallen into their hands?'

> From a conversation between Hugo Ganz, an Austrian observer, and a senior Russian official who had asked to remain anonymous; H. Ganz, *The Downfall of Russia*, 1904, in A. Nove, *An Economic History of the U.S.S.R.*, 1976, p 27

Questions

a (i) What do you understand by the 'terror from above' and 'terror from below' (lines 2—3)? In what way does the Russian official see them as connected?

    (ii) Explain 'the fatal policy which is ruining the country' (line 10); 'to repudiate our debts' (line 12); 'the state kitchen' (line 17).

    (iii) In what ways does the official criticise Russian autocracy and what problems does he see for a peaceful transfer to a constitutional form of government (lines 17—21)?

    (iv) Explain the significance of lines 28—30.

b Why do you think the Russian official and, by extension, the Russian bureaucracy, viewed the 'future of this country in the darkest terms' (line 9)?

c How did the official see the 'catastrophe' occurring?

* d In what ways were the fears of the official realised in the 1905—6 period and how far do you think his assertion (lines 20—21) that the

autocracy would not 'voluntarily yield without external pressure' to liberal forces was borne out in the constitutional experiments of 1906–17?

e What remedy do you think the official provides for Russia's ills and what does he see as the cause of them?

* f 'The basic weakness of Russia in the period before the 1917 Revolutions lay in her lack of an efficient bureaucracy in an increasingly industrialising situation.' Discuss.

2 War – the Initial Response

What had happened? Only a month or three weeks ago no thinking Russian citizen had doubted the fact that the ruler of Russia was a despicable individual, unworthy of serious mention; no one would have dreamed of quoting him except as a joke. Yet in a matter of days
5 everything had changed. Quite voluntarily, seemingly educated people would gather with serious faces around the advertisement pillars, and the Tsar's long string of pompous titles, simply because they were printed on these massive cylindrical slabs, did not strike them as ridiculous at all. Equally voluntarily, people would of their own accord read out in loud,
10 clear voices: 'At the call to arms Russia has risen to meet the enemy, with iron in her hands and the cross upon her heart, not for martial ambition nor for the sake of vain earthly glory, but for a just cause – to defend the integrity and safety of our divinely-protected Empire. . . .'

Throughout her long journey Vanya had observed the effects of war –
15 the loading of troop-trains, the farewells. Especially at small stations, the Russian leave-taking was an almost joyous affair, with the reservists dancing away to balalaika music and raising the dust on the trampled earth of the trackside. . . . And no one demonstrated against the Tsar.

Now Sanya was equally unable to answer her question: 'What has
20 happened?' He too felt himself being sucked by the same whirlpool into the same bottomless pit. . . . The decades of 'civic' literature, the ideals of the intelligentsia, the students' devotion to the common people – was all this to be abandoned and cast aside in a single moment? Could they simply forget it all? . . . The ideas of Lavrov, of Mikhailovsky?
25 . . . Hadn't he himself once said? . . . Anyone watching them might have thought that she was the militant patriot of the two, and that it was he who was gently arguing against the war. . . . Sanya lowered his newspapers. He was lost for words and began to justify himself with some embarrassment.

30 'It's not like the Japanese war. They attacked us. What have we done to the Germans?'

A fine thing – giving way to that reactionary sort of patriotism! It was a betrayal of all his principles. All right, so he never was a revolutionary, but he was always a pacifist.

35 The newspapers resting on his knees, Sanya quietly folded his arms.

Unable to defend himself, he stared placidly at her and nodded his head. He felt sad.

Terrified by his silence, she guessed what was in his mind.

'You aren't going to volunteer now, are you?' Sanya nodded. He
40 smiled diffidently.

'I feel . . . sorry for Russia.'

Alexander Solzhenitsyn, *August 1914*, 1972, pp 14–15

Questions

a   (i)   Why do you think 'no thinking Russian citizen had doubted the
          fact that the ruler of Russia was a despicable individual' (lines 1–
          3)? In what ways did this attitude change once war broke out?

   (ii)   What were 'The decades of "civic" literature, the ideals of the
          intelligentsia, the students' devotion to the common people'
          (lines 21–2)? Why do you think they were cast aside in 1914?

   (iii) What were the 'ideas of Lavrov, of Mikhailovsky' (line 24)?

   (iv)   Explain the reference to the 'Japanese war' and suggest in what
          ways the German war was different (lines 30–1)?

* b   Who is Alexander Solzhenitsyn and how reliable do you think this
       passage is as a piece of historical evidence?

   c   Is it possible to explain why patriotism made such an impact upon
       Russia in the early part of the war?

* d   The revolutionary ideals current in Russia in 1914 did not have the
       same power as patriotism in arousing people to action. Discuss.

3   The Changing Attitudes towards the War – a Police View

The exceptional importance of the present historical moment . . .
dictates the necessity of urgent and exhaustive measures for the
elimination of the prevailing disorder and the clearing up of the
atmosphere of public discontent. Lack of determination in decisions and
5 casual half-measures, as have been proved by recent experiences, are
inadmissable. They do not solve the problem. They merely add to the
already strained relations between the Government and the
people . . . and pave the way for the wildest outbursts at the first
opportunity. . . . The summer campaign of 1915 ended the noisy and
10 constant manifestations of chauvinist enthusiasm seen in the early days of
the War, and brought to light the hopeless inadequacy of theoretical
peace-time calculations when applied to the immensities of modern war.
Military reverses brought the masses to a clearer understanding of the
problems of war and the danger there may be in the disorganisation of the
15 rear. But here, again, the officially proclaimed and generally accepted
watchword 'all for victory' forced the country to seek a way out of its

difficulties in new energetic and urgent measures for the welfare of the army . . . which were harmful to that stability in the rear upon which, in the last resort, depends the issue of the War. . . .

20 The brilliant success of the offensive of General Brusilov in the spring of the present year and the current solution to the problem of supplying the troops proved convincingly that the task undertaken by the Government and the community has been fulfilled more than successfully. The question of the organization of the army supply may be held to have been satisfactorily settled . . . But, on the other hand, the 25 disintegration of the rear, that is of the whole country, which is now steadily increasing has to-day reached such monstrous and extreme form that it has begun to be a menace to the success obtained at the front, and in the very near future promises to throw the country into chaotic, spontaneous and catastrophic anarchy.

30 . . . all these things have led to an unfair distribution of foodstuffs and articles of prime necessity, an immense and rapid increase in the cost of living, and to inadequacy in sources of supply and means of existence. These factors show that the neglect of the rear is the prime cause of the disorganization of the huge machine of the State, and also contain 35 categorical evidence that a terrible crisis is already on the way and that it must be met in either one way or the other.

The above analysis is entirely confirmed by the extreme anxiety which may be observed everywhere. At the beginning of the present month, September, exceptionally strong feelings of opposition and hostility to 40 the Government were in evidence in every section of the capital's population. . . . Now, by the end of the month, these hostile feelings, according to reliable evidence, have attained a power among the masses which was without precedent even in 1905—1906. Openly and without restraint there are complaints of the 'dishonesty of the administration', 45 the unbearable burden of the War, the impossible conditions of everyday life. The inflammable statements of the radicals, and other elements of the Left to the effect that one must 'first get rid of the Germans at home, and then proceed against those abroad' are meeting more and more approval.

There is little doubt that rumours that Russia is on the eve of a 50 revolution are exaggerated as compared to the actual conditions, but nevertheless the situation is serious enough to deserve immediate attention.

> Petrograd police report for October 1916, in response to the Minister of the Interior's circular of 1915 asking local police for monthly information on the political situation; in *Krasni Arkhiv*, XVII, pp 3—35

Questions

a (i) Discuss why 'Lack of determination in decisions and casual half-measures' failed to 'solve the problem' (lines 4—6); why the summer campaign of 1915 ended 'chauvinist enthusiasm' (line 10).

(ii) Explain the 'new energetic and urgent measures for the welfare of the army' (lines 17–18); 'the brilliant success of the offensive of General Brusilov' (line 19).

(iii) What threat did the 'disintegration of the rear' (line 25) pose in 1916?

(iv) Why do you think the authors referred back to the events of 1905–6 (lines 41–3)?

(v) Who were the 'Germans at home' (line 47) and why was it necessary to defeat them before it was possible to 'proceed against those abroad'?

b What relationship did the authors of this report see between war, even when waged successfully, and public disorder?

c In what ways did Russia underestimate the nature of modern warfare and with what consequences for her armed forces?

d The report concludes with a statement of cautious optimism. If you had been a Russian official and had read it what would your reaction have been?

* e The Revolutions of 1917 were caused directly by Russian involvement in a war the consequences of which were not understood by Government but were borne by the masses. Once the burden became unbearable, radical changes began to occur. Explain.

4   The Sealed Train

31 MARCH   Berlin
(Memo by an official of the Foreign Ministry with the General Staff.)
    . . . Above all we must avoid compromising the travellers by excessive attentiveness on our part. It would be very desirable to have some sort of
5 declaration from the Swiss government. If we suddenly send these restless elements to Sweden without such a declaration it may be used against us.
31 MARCH
(Assistant Secretary von Stumm to Ambassador Romberg in Bern. In Cipher.)
10   Urgent! The journey of the Russian émigres through Germany should take place very quickly, since the Entente has already started counter-measures in Switzerland. Speed up the negotiations as much as possible.
2 APRIL
15 (Count von Brockdorff-Rantzau, German Ambassador in Copenhagen, to the Ministry of Foreign Affairs. Top Secret)
    . . . We must now definitely try to create the utmost chaos in Russia. To this end we must avoid any discernible influence in the course of the Russian revolution. But we must secretly do all we can to aggravate the
20 contradictions between the moderate and the extreme parties, since we are extremely interested in the victory of the latter, for another upheaval will then be inevitable, and will take forms which will shake the Russian state to its foundations. . . .

Support by us of the extreme element is preferable, because in this way
25 the work is done more thoroughly and achieves its results more quickly.
According to all forecasts we may count on the disintegration being so far
advanced in three months or so that military intervention by us will
guarantee the collapse of Russian might.

Alexander Solzhenitsyn, *Lenin in Zurich*, 1978, pp 214–15

The man [Kerensky] who loomed so large in March was to be seen in
30 retrospect as a Hamlet of the Russian Revolution. But then the
Revolution had many Hamlets and only one serious candidate for
dictator.

He was at the time writhing with impatience in Switzerland. Lenin's
original analysis of the Revolution – a plot by the French and British
35 embassies to prevent a separate peace – soon gave way to a more realistic
recognition of its elemental character. Yet the news, much as it was
exhilarating, was also infuriating. Everything was wonderful, but
everything seemed to go wrong. It was an automatic reflex for him to
exclaim that the Mensheviks and Social Revolutionaries were betraying
40 the proletariat. Yet it was not quite clear what the Bolsheviks were
doing. . . . His eagerness to return to Russia turned into a frenzy at the
news of what was happening to the Bolshevik organization at
home. . . . To Lenin's dismay (even though he himself had not worked
out fully an alternative policy), the new arrivals [Stalin and Kamenev had
45 just returned from Siberia] adopted a conciliatory policy towards the
Mensheviks, and even, o horror! towards the Provisional
Government. . . . He was supremely confident that once in Russia he
could redirect his straying cohorts, but he had to get there and fast.

But how? France, England and Italy were not going to facilitate
50 passage through their territory of a man who believed that the imperialist
war should be turned into a civil one. Those Russian revolutionaries who
believed in the prosecution of the war, like Plekhanov, were given every
encouragement and help to return to Russia. But Lenin and many others
were known to be, to put it mildly, not friendly to the Allied
55 cause. . . . Ever since the beginning of the war the German Imperial
Government and the General Staff had been conscious of the great help
they might derive from the Russian revolutionary movement. Internal
subversion of the enemy was already recognised as a legitimate weapon of
warfare. And in the case of Russia the opportunities for its use appeared
60 limitless. . . . Granted Lenin's premises, his decision to accept German
help was perfectly natural. It was not to affect his position an iota: he was
working to bring about a new revolution in Russia, but that government
in turn was to overthrow the German government and bring about the
victory of revolutionary socialism in all Europe. . . . Thus on April 9
65 [1917] Lenin, his wife, and more than twenty leading members of his
Swiss group, including the Zinovievs and Inessa Armand, set out for
home. After Germany they travelled through Sweden, then Finland.
. . . At 11.10 the night of April 3 the train pulled in at the Finland Station

of Petrograd. Vladimir Ilyich was home. . . . To the strains of the
70 'Marseillaise' (the Russian bands had not yet learned the 'International' so
the 'Marseillaise' had to do though it was, alas, not only a revolutionary
hymn but the anthem of 'French imperialism'), Lenin descended from his
car and was engulfed by the greeters.

Adam B. Ulam, *Lenin and the Bolsheviks*, 1978, pp 422−9

Questions

a (i)   Why was it very important for the Germans to 'avoid
compromising the travellers' (line 3)?

(ii) Who were the 'Russian émigres' and what was the 'Entente'
(lines 10−11)?

(iii) Why was it to Germany's advantage to try 'to create the
utmost chaos in Russia' (line 17)?

(iv) What were 'the contradictions between the moderate and the
extreme parties' (lines 20−21) and why did Germany want the
latter to win?

(v)   Who were 'the Mensheviks and Social Revolutionaries' (line
39) and what was Lenin's attitude to them and why?

(vi) What conciliatory policy did Stalin and Kamenev adopt in
early 1917 (lines 44−7)?

(vii) Why did Lenin believe that 'the imperialist war should be
turned into a civil one' (lines 50−1)?

(viii) Explain the significance of lines 61−4.

(ix) What are the 'International' and the 'Marseillaise' (lines 69−
72), and why are they important to left-wing politics?

b Why did the German government want to get Lenin back to Russia?

* c 'Internal subversion of the enemy was already recognised as a
legitimate weapon of warfare' (lines 57−9). Discuss.

* d How justifiable do you think it is to call Kerensky 'a Hamlet of the
Russian Revolution' (line 30)?

* e 'To be, or not to be. That is the question.' How far do you think that
Shakespeare's famous line sums up the uncertainties of the Bolsheviks
in 1917?

5 Revolution − the Historian's View

The source of the catastrophe which overcame the Empire may,
undoubtedly, be traced far back into the history of the Russian people. As
long as the country was not asked to make the supreme and heroic effort
imposed upon it by the War, it managed to trail, and not without a
5 certain degree of success, behind the other European countries along the
road of economic development and progress. But the Great War put
the whole framework of the Empire to a severe test. The obsoleteness and
the imperfections of its political, social and economic structure could no

longer be concealed and ignored. Following the example of England, France and Germany, who, reacting from the blows they were receiving, made superhuman efforts to meet the emergency, Russia, or rather her educated classes, tried to organise their country for the War; but their efforts were sporadic, uncoordinated, and almost pathetic in their helplessness. A ship without a captain and manned by an unskilled and undisciplined crew, Russia drifted along an uncharted course.

Few are the instances in the history of the human race when the impotence and inadequacy of a political regime revealed themselves with such striking force. The Emperor was a weak and obstinate man, a mere tool in the hands of an unbalanced woman guided by vulgar adventurers. The bureaucracy was senile, unadaptable and helpless in the emergency. It soon lost whatever virtues it might have possessed before the War. The Duma was sadly lacking in authority and leadership. The educated classes, in spite of their honest desire to champion the cause of the people, were crippled by the opposition of the bureaucracy and their aloofness from the masses. There was no organised labour, no real self-government on a broad democratic basis, no real tradition of public service. The economic and educational standards of the masses were appallingly low. And beneath the thin layer of refined European culture one could feel the subdued, heavy breathing of the millions of peasants, inarticulate, ignored and often forgotten in their snow-clad cottages in the immensity of the Russian plains. The menacing murmur which rose at times from the countryside reminded those in power that everything was not well. . . .

The War – the losses in men, territory, and wealth, the economic hardships, the flagrant impotence of the ruling clique when faced with crisis, the degeneration of autocracy itself – all brought to the top the powers of discontent and social antagonism which had been gathering beneath the ominously quiet and peaceful surface. Who will be bold enough to determine which was the factor that played the leading part in bringing about the Revolution? Was it the folly of the Emperor and the Empress? the decay of the Government? military losses? the secular grievances of the peasants? the starving conditions of the cities? the weariness with the war? We cannot answer these questions, just as there is no way of determining which of the many streams pouring into a river is responsible for the breaking of the dam and the flooding of the country below, or which handful of snow started the avalanche that buries in its deadly path the villages and pastures of the hard-working mountaineers. One thing, however, is clear. When the swollen river breaks the dam or the avalanche begins its descent into the valley, there is no human power which can stop it until the elementary forces of nature over which men have no control have exhausted their destructive energies. The same may be said of the Russian Revolution. Here the landslide which started in March 1917, did not reach the bottom of the valley until the establishment of the Soviet rule.

M. T. Florinsky, *The End of the Russian Empire*, 1976, pp 246–8

Questions

a (i) Why does Florinsky say that Russia had taken some steps along the road of progress that were 'not without a certain degree of success' (lines 4–5)?

   (ii) In what ways was the social, political and economic structure of Russia obsolete (lines 7–9)?

   (iii) Explain the use of the metaphor in lines 14–15.

   (iv) 'The Duma was sadly lacking in authority and leadership' (lines 21–2). Why was this?

   (v) Explain Florinsky's reference to elemental forces beneath the veneer of European culture (lines 27–31).

b In what ways were the inadequacies of the Russian political system revealed by the war?

c What methodological point does Florinsky make about the difficulty of prescribing an exact causation for the Russian Revolution?

* d Florinsky's conclusion that events in Russia in 1917 had a naturalistic character and implied a process in some ways inevitable once started is misleading. How would you answer this criticism?

Further Work

a The same patriotic fervour that occurred in Russia in 1914 also occurred in Britain. Why did Russia have a revolution and Britain not?

b Personality rather than principle is the key to the fullest understanding of the Russian Revolution. Discuss.

c The causes of the revolution in 1917 were almost entirely economic. How far do you think this statement is justifiable?

d The historian's function is to explain the past. This means making the past ordered and logical. In this process the ideas of causation and consequence play a crucial role. Is this true?

e Events are essentially multi-causal. To identify and give prominence to one major cause is misleading but may be necessary if the historian is to do his job properly. Discuss.

IV   Lenin and Stalin – The Character of Stalinism

Introduction

Winston Churchill once referred to Russia as 'a riddle wrapped in a mystery inside an enigma'. He could have been speaking of Stalin who, of all of the great leaders of the twentieth century, is the most difficult for the historian to understand, or to see as an individual in isolation from the processes which brought him to power. Only Solzhenitsyn in *The First Circle* provides a convincing picture of Stalin's personality. As a result, this section is not concerned with Stalin's personality but with the character of Stalinism; is it correct to see Stalinism as a fundamental part of the development of Soviet Communism or does it signify a political dead-end?

By mid 1920 the nascent Soviet state had triumphed in the civil war although at a terrible cost. The war had utterly disrupted the Russian economy and had stifled the dynamism of proletarian democracy. The Tenth Party Congress of March 1921, coinciding with the Kronstadt Mutiny, marked the end of democracy for the proletariat. The Resolution on Party Unity made it clear that power was to lie with the Party and that any form of factionalism would be ruthlessly eliminated. This marks the beginning of repression which would be taken to its peak in the purges of the 1930s and 1940s. Stalin followed up Lenin's position in 1928 with his emphasis placed firmly on 'iron discipline'.

Trotsky saw Stalinism as a consequence of processes begun under Lenin, a view which is echoed by Lucio Colletti. The Party may have retained a vigorous life during the civil war but the development of the New Economic Policy from 1921 led to a massive expansion of the bureaucracy. It was this development which both Trotsky and Colletti saw as crucial to understanding the success of Stalinism, and as an inevitable part of the process of revolutions.

It was perhaps because Stalin did not have such a charismatic personality as Lenin that it became important to develop the 'cult of the individual' which Khrushchev first criticised in his speech in 1956. In fact the leader has always played an important rôle in Soviet politics but within a framework of collegiality. Stalinism could not be made to work in such a situation. Rivals, either actual or suspected, had to be ruthlessly eliminated. The purges of the 1930s and 1940s have their origins in this premise. The assassination of Kirov in late 1934 provided the catalyst and has been seen by some historians as the watershed of Stalin's rule. But, as Merle Fainsod has shown, the basic formula of Stalinist totalitarianism existed before then. 'The revolution from above' began in economic, social and cultural affairs in the late 1920s, first with the collectivisation of agriculture and then the westernisation of industry. Stalin dragged Russia into the twentieth century, but at a high cost in terms of lives, and principles.

In doing this Stalin was continuing a process, begun by Lenin, which still persists in the Soviet policies of today. Stalinism had no place for a creative Party and in that sense it marked a political dead-end. The role of the Party in Russia was rapidly restored after 1953. The process of de-Stalinisation began in 1956 but it was halted in the late 1960s. Stalin may no longer be buried in the Kremlin but the bureaucratisation of politics that epitomised Stalinism still persists. The legacy of Stalin remains largely intact.

Further Reading

E. H. Carr, *A History of Soviet Russia*, in 14 volumes, Macmillan 1950–78, covers the period to 1930 in depth.

Robert Conquest, *The Great Terror*, Penguin, 1971, the best study of the purges.

I. Deutscher, *Stalin – a Political Biography*, 2nd. edn, Pelican, 1966, the best biography.

I. Deutscher, *A Trotsky Trilogy*: *The Prophet Armed* (1954), *The Prophet Unarmed* (1959), *The Prophet Outcast* (1963), Pelican, an excellent study.

I. Howe, *Trotsky*, Fontana, 1978, a convenient, brief study of his ideas and life.

Alec Nove, *Stalinism and After*, Allen and Unwin, 1976, a good general account.

A. Solzhenitsyn, *The Gulag Archipelago*, Fontana, 1974–8, a gripping study of the process of repression.

A. Ulam, *Stalin: The Man and his Era*, Allen Lane, 1974, an imaginative and stimulating study.

See also the books by Lionel Kochan, T. P. Nettl and Alec Nove, cited in the bibliography of chapter III.

1   The Party and Opposition

1. The congress calls the attention of all members of the Party to the fact that the unity and cohesion of the ranks of the Party, the guarantee of complete mutual confidence among Party members and genuine team-work that really embodies the unanimity of will of the vanguard of the proletariat, are particularly essential at the present time, when a number of circumstances are increasing the vacillation among the petty-bourgeois population of the country.

2. Notwithstanding this, even before the general Party discussion on the trade unions, certain signs of factionalism had been apparent in the Party — the formation of groups with separate platforms, striving to a certain degree to segregate and create their own group discipline. . . . All class-conscious workers must clearly realise that factionalism of any kind is harmful and impermissible, for no matter how members of individual groups may desire to safeguard Party unity, factionalism in practice inevitably leads to the weakening of team-work and to intensified and repeated attempts by the enemies of the governing Party, who have wormed their way into it, to widen the cleavage and to use it for counter-revolutionary purposes.

The way the enemies of the proletariat take advantage of every deviation from a thoroughly consistent communist line was perhaps most strikingly shown in the case of the Kronstadt mutiny, when the bourgeois counter-revolutionaries and whiteguards in all countries of the world immediately expressed their readiness to accept the slogans of the Soviet system, if only they might thereby secure the overthrow of the dictatorship of the proletariat in Russia, and when the Socialist-Revolutionaries and the bourgeois counter-revolutionaries in general resorted in Kronstadt to slogans calling for an insurrection against the Soviet Government of Russia ostensibly in the interest of the Soviet power. . . .

4. In the practical struggle against factionalism, every organisation of the Party must take strict measures to prevent all factional actions. Criticism of the Party's shortcomings, which is absolutely necessary, must be conducted in such a way that every practical proposal shall be submitted immediately, without any delay, in the most precise form possible, for consideration and decision to the leading local and central bodies of the Party. . . .

6. The congress, therefore, hereby declares dissolved and orders the immediate dissolution of all groups without exception formed on the basis of one platform or another (such as the Workers' Opposition group, the Democratic Centralism group, etc.). Non-observance of this decision of the congress shall entail unconditional and instant expulsion from the Party.

> Preliminary Draft Resolution of the Tenth Party Congress on Party Unity, March 1921, in V. I. Lenin, *Selected Works*, 1975, pp 625–8

The achievement and maintenance of the dictatorship of the proletariat is impossible without a party which is strong by reason of its solidarity and iron discipline. But iron discipline in the Party is inconceivable without unity of will, without complete and absolute unity of action on the part of all members of the Party. This does not mean, of course, that the possibility of contests of opinion within the Party is thereby precluded. On the contrary, iron discipline does not preclude but presupposes criticism and contest of opinion within the Party. Least of all does it mean that discipline must be 'blind'. On the contrary, iron discipline does not preclude but presupposes conscious and voluntary submission, for only conscious discipline can be truly iron discipline. But after a contest of opinion has been closed, after criticism has been exhausted and a decision has been arrived at, unity of will and unity of action of all Party members are the necessary conditions without which neither Party unity nor iron discipline in the Party is conceivable . . . from this it follows that the existence of factions is incompatible either with the Party's unity or with its iron discipline. It need hardly be proved that the existence of factions leads to the existence of a number of centres, and the existence of a number of centres connotes the absence of one common centre in the Party, the breaking up of the unity of will, the weakening and disintegration of discipline, the weakening and disintegration of the dictatorship.

> A statement by Stalin on the position of the Party, in his lectures 'The Foundations of Leninism', 1924; in J. Stalin, *Problems of Leninism*, 1947, pp 89–90

Questions

a (i) What did Lenin mean by 'the vanguard of the proletariat' (lines 4–5); 'the petty-bourgeois' (line 6); 'counter-revolutionary purposes' (lines 17–18); 'the dictatorship of the proletariat' (line 25)?
   (ii) Explain the reference to 'certain signs of factionalism' (line 9); 'the Kronstadt mutiny' (line 21).
   (iii) What did Stalin mean in lines 58–62?
b Why did Lenin not attack the issue of factionalism before 1921?
c The 1921 Party Congress can be characterised in two ways. It saw the end of democracy within the Party but also saw the emergence of the New Economic Policy with its seeming betrayal of socialist principles. Do you think this was intentional?
d How far does Stalin's statement about the character of the Party follow on from the Leninist position?
* e Examine the causes, course and consequences of the Kronstadt mutiny. Did it pose an effective challenge to the Soviet state?
* f Lenin created the Party and Stalin destroyed it. Discuss.

2   Stalinism – Causes?

It is sufficiently well known that every revolution up to this time has been followed by a reaction, or even counter-revolution. This, to be sure, has never thrown the nation all the way back to its starting point, but it has always taken from the people the lion's share of their conquests. The victims of the first reactionary wave have been, as a general rule, those pioneers, initiators and instigators who stood at the head of the masses in the period of revolutionary offensive. In their stead people of the second line, in league with former enemies of the revolution, have been advanced to the front. . . .

It would be naïve to imagine that Stalin, previously unknown to the
masses, suddenly issued from the wings fully armed with a complete
strategical plan. No indeed. Before he felt out his own course, the
bureaucracy felt out Stalin himself. He brought it all the necessary
guarantees: the prestige of an old Bolshevik, a strong character, narrow
vision, and close bonds with the political machine as the sole source of his
influence. The success which fell upon him was at first a surprise to Stalin
himself. It was the friendly welcome of the new ruling group, trying to
free itself from the old principles and from the control of the masses, and
having need of a reliable arbiter in its inner affairs. A secondary figure
before the masses and in the events of the revolution, Stalin revealed
himself as the indubitable leader of the Thermidorian bureaucracy, as first
in its midst. . . .

We have defined the Soviet Thermidor as a triumph of the bureaucracy over the masses. We have tried to disclose the historic conditions of
this triumph. The revolutionary vanguard of the proletariat was in part
devoured by the administrative apparatus and gradually demoralized, in
part annihilated in the civil war, and in part thrown out and crushed. The
tired and disappointed masses were indifferent to what was happening on
the summits. . . .

The basis of bureaucratic rule is the poverty of society in objects of
consumption, with the resulting struggle of each against all. When there
is enough goods in a store the purchasers can come whenever they want
to. When there is little goods the purchasers are compelled to stand in line.
When the lines are very long, it is necessary to appoint a policeman to
keep order. Such is the starting point of the power of the Soviet
bureaucracy. It 'knows' who is to get something and who has to
wait. . . .

But that is not the sole reason. Alongside the economic factor dictating
capitalistic methods of payment at the present stage, there operates a
parallel political factor in the person of the bureaucracy itself. In its very
essence it is the planter and protector of inequality. It arose in the
beginning as the bourgeois organ of a workers' State. In establishing and
defending the advantages of a minority, it of course draws off the cream
for its own use. Nobody who has wealth to distribute ever omits himself.
Thus out of a social necessity there has developed an organ which has far
outgrown its socially necessary function, and become an independent
factor and therewith the source of great danger for the whole social
organism.

The social meaning of the Soviet Thermidor now begins to take form
before us. The poverty and cultural backwardness of the masses has again
become incarnate in the malignant figure of the ruler with a great club in
his hand. The deposed and abused bureaucracy . . . has again become its
lord. On this road it has attained such a degree of social and moral
alienation from the popular masses, that it cannot now permit any control
over either its activities or its income.

Leon Trotsky, *The Revolution Betrayed*, 1937, pp 83, 93, 104,
110—12

Questions

a (i) What did Trotsky mean by 'It is sufficiently well known . . . or even counter-revolution' (lines 1 – 2)?

(ii) Trotsky saw Stalin's 'close bonds with the political machine as the sole source of his influence' (lines 15 – 16). How true was this?

(iii) How was 'the new ruling group trying to free itself from the old principles and from the control of the masses' (lines 17 – 18)?

(iv) Explain what Trotsky meant by 'the Thermidorian bureaucracy' (line 21); 'The revolutionary vanguard of the proletariat' (line 25)

(v) What did Trotsky see as the 'basis of bureaucratic rule' (line 30)?

b Who was Trotsky and what part did he play in Soviet history to his death in 1940?

c How reliable do you think Trotsky's analysis of the causes of Stalinism is?

d What are Trotsky's basic criticisms of the bureaucratisation of the Soviet political machine? From what you know about the 1925 to 1941 period how valid do you think these criticisms are?

* *e* Trotsky's analysis of the development of the Soviet state emphasises processes rather than people. How true is this?

* *f* Explain why it was Stalin and not Trotsky who won the succession after Lenin's death.

3   Stalin Denounced

. . . After Stalin's death the Central Committee of the Party began to implement a policy of explaining concisely and consistently that it is impermissible and foreign to the spirit of Marxism – Leninism to elevate one person, to transform him into a superman possessing supernatural
5 characteristics akin to those of a god. Such a man supposedly knows everything, sees everything, thinks for everyone, can do anything, is infallible in his behaviour. . . . The great modesty of the genius of the revolution, Vladimir Ilyich Lenin, is known. Lenin had always stressed the role of the people as the creator of history, the directing and
10 organizational role of the Party as a living and creative organism, and also the role of the Central Committee.

Marxism does not negate the role of the leaders of the workers' class in directing the revolutionary liberation movement.

While ascribing great importance to the roles of the leaders and
15 organizers of the masses, Lenin at the same time mercilessly stigmatized every manifestation of the cult of the individual, inexorably combated the foreign-to-Marxism views about a 'hero' and a 'crowd' and countered all efforts to oppose a 'hero' to the masses and to the people. . . .
20 Lenin resolutely stood against every attempt aimed at belittling or weakening the directing role of the Party in the structure of the Soviet

State. He worked out Bolshevik principles of Party direction and norms of Party life, stressing that the guiding principle of Party leadership is its collegiality. . . .

25   It was precisely during this period [1935–1937–1938] that the practice of mass repression through the government apparatus was born, first against the enemies of Leninism – Trotskyites, Zinovievites, Bukharinites, long since politically defeated by the Party, and subsequently also against many honest Communists. . . . Stalin originated
30 the concept 'enemy of the people'. This term automatically rendered it unnecessary that the ideological errors of a man or men engaged in a controversy be proven; this term made possible the usage of the most cruel repression, violating all norms of revolutionary legality, against anyone who in any way disagreed with Stalin, against those who were
35 only suspected of hostile intent, against those who had bad reputations. . . .

    Lenin used severe methods only in the most necessary cases, when the exploiting classes were still in existence and were vigorously opposing the revolution, when the struggle for survival was decidedly assuming the
40 sharpest forms, even including a civil war.

    Stalin, on the other hand, used extreme methods and mass repression at a time when the revolution was already victorious, when the Soviet state was strengthened, when the exploiting classes were already liquidated and Socialist relations were rooted solidly in all phases of national
45 economy, when our Party was politically consolidated and had strengthened itself both numerically and ideologically. Instead of proving his political correctness and mobilizing the masses, he often chose the path of repression and physical annihilation, not only against actual enemies, but also against individuals who had not committed any crimes against
50 the Party and the Soviet government. . . .

    It was determined that of the 139 members and candidates of the Party's Central Committee who were elected at the XVIIth Congress, ninety-eight persons, i.e. 70 per cent, were arrested and shot [mostly in 1937 and 1938]. (Indignation in the hall.). . . . The same fate met not
55 only the Central Committee members but also the majority of the delegates to the XVIIth Party Congress. Of 1,966 delegates with either voting or advisory rights, 1,108 persons were arrested on charges of anti-revolutionary crimes. . . .

    Facts prove that many abuses were made on Stalin's orders without
60 reckoning with any norms of Party and Soviet legality. Stalin was a very distrustful man, sickly suspicious; we knew this from our work with him. He could look at a man and say: 'Why are your eyes so shifty today?' or 'Why are you turning so much today and avoiding to look me directly in the eyes?' . . . Possessing unlimited power he indulged in great wilful-
65 ness and choked a person morally and physically. A situation was created where one could not express one's own will.

    When Stalin said that one or another should be arrested, it was necessary to accept on faith that he was an 'enemy of the people'.

Meanwhile, Beria's gang, which ran the organs of state security, outdid
70 itself in proving the guilt of the arrested and the truth of materials which it
falsified. . . .

> From the Secret Speech on the crimes of Stalin, delivered by
> Nikita Khrushchev to the Twentieth Party Congress, February
> 1956; in N. Khrushchev, *Khrushchev Remembers*, vol I, 1977, pp
> 580–2, 587, 591, 607–8

Questions

a (i)   What is 'the Central Committee of the Party' (line 1)?
   (ii) What light do lines 8–11 throw on Lenin's ideological
         position?
   (iii) What did Lenin mean by the 'cult of the individual' (line 16); 'the
         guiding principle of Party leadership is its collegiality' (lines
         23–4)?
   (iv) Explain the meaning of the 'enemies of Leninism . . .' (line 27)
         and 'Stalin originated the concept "enemy of the people"' (lines
         29–30).
   (v)   What was 'Beria's gang' (line 69)?

b Who was Nikita Khrushchev and what role did he play in Soviet
   politics?

c Why does Khrushchev compare Stalin with Lenin?

d What picture of Stalin's personality emerged in the speech?

* e What effects have the programme of 'De-Stalinisation' had upon the
   way historians view Stalin?

* f The basic difference between Lenin and Stalin was that the former
   accepted that his actions required some legal basis whereas Stalin did
   not. Do you agree?

* g It is paradoxical that it is Lenin who has become a cult figure in Soviet
   society and not Stalin. Discuss.

4   The Formula of Stalin's Totalitarianism

The organization of the economy and society to maximize industrial and
military strength involved a strengthening of the totalitarian features of
the regime. 'The revolution from above' which was imposed on the
peasantry and the cuts in consumption which 'primitive socialist
5 accumulation' demanded could not be achieved without increasing resort
to compulsion. The consolidation of Stalin's absolute power, the ruthless
purge of party dissidents, the strengthening of the bureaucratic and
hierarchical features of the regime, the expansion in the role of the secret
police, and the rise of forced labour advanced hand in hand with forced-
10 draft industrialization and militarization.

The formula of totalitarian rule as it took shape under Stalin's
ministrations was a complex one. It represented, in one aspect, a drive to

safeguard his own security by obliterating all actual or potential competing centres of power. Positively, it tried to saturate and paralyse the minds of the Soviet populace with a monolithic stream of agitation and propaganda stressing the superiority of the Soviet system and the virtues of its leaders. Negatively, it sought to deny the people access to any alternative by cutting them off from the outside world and from each other. Through the secret police, it attempted to create a milieu of pervasive insecurity founded on the ever-present fear of the informer and the labour camp. . . . In this system of institutionalized mutual suspicion, the competing hierarchies of Party, army and administration were kept in purposeful conflict and provided no point of final resolution short of Stalin and his trusted henchmen in the Politburo. The concentration of power in Stalin's hands rested on the dispersal of power among his subordinates.

In another of its aspects, the Stalinist formula sought to come to terms with the demands of industrialization. It enlisted the new Soviet intelligentsia in its service and rewarded the elite among them with high material privileges and elevated social status. It created a labour aristocracy of honoured Stakhanovites to serve as the bellwether of the working class. . . .

In order to consolidate his position as the leader of the party of order in Soviet society, Stalin also endeavoured to identify totalitarian rule with the forces of tradition and respectability in Russian life. . . . It led him to a drastic reorganization of the educational system, the abandonment of its early experimental and progressive features, and its transformation into an authoritarian instrument to instill devotion to the regime and to prepare youth for their appointed roles in the Soviet hierarchical structure. . . . It produced an uneasy de facto 'concordat' with the church in which the political loyalty of the clergy and their communicants was exchanged for a precarious toleration of religious practices. It expressed itself in a striking rehabilitation of patriotism as the cohesive force of Soviet society and sought to present the Soviet regime as the legitimate heir of the best of the Russian past. It induced a new emphasis on law as an instrument to enforce the responsibility of the subject to the state and to introduce rationality and order in the relations among state enterprises and individuals.

The drive to stabilize the regime's authority was accompanied by a profound reorientation in Soviet ideology directed towards the exaltation of statism. The theory of the withering away of the state was all but repudiated. The primacy of base over superstructure, one of the hallowed Marxist orthodoxies, was in fact reversed and the determining influence of environment minimized. The state superstructure was glorified and magnified as the creative source of all initiative and direction in Soviet society. The role of the individual was redefined in terms of conscious, disciplined subordination to state purposes.

This remarkable development has its parallels in the natural history of other revolutions. Every revolutionary movement undertakes to con-

60 solidate its authority after it has won power and exhausted the dynamic
momentum of its programme. Even the most authoritarian of regimes
cannot evade the problem of coming to terms with its environment. The
price of survival involves the abandonment of utopian goals which
cannot be realized, the repudiation of orthodoxies which were previously
65 sacrosanct, and the adoption of expedients which offend the most
treasured dogmas of the original revolutionary programme. The most
ironical chapters of revolutionary history are its unintended consequences.

Merle Fainsod, *How Russia is Ruled*, 1963, pp 109–11

Questions

a (i) What was 'The revolution from above' and how was it achieved
in Stalinist Russia (line 3)?

(ii) How far do you think Fainsod is correct in her assertion that one
aspect of the totalitarian rule of Stalin was 'a drive to
safeguard . . . centres of power' (lines 12–14)?

(iii) What was the Politburo (line 24)?

(iv) What does Fainsod mean by 'The concentration of
power . . . among his subordinates' (lines 24–6)?

(v) What was the 'labour aristocracy of honoured Stakhanovites'
(lines 30–1) and why were they important to Stalin?

(vi) What is meant by 'statism' (line 51); 'the theory of the withering
away of the state' (line 51); 'the primacy of base over
superstructure' (line 52)?

b What does the author see as the positive and negative characteristics of
the totalitarian formula?

c Why did Stalin endeavour 'to identify totalitarian rule with the forces
of tradition and respectability in Russian life' (lines 34–5)? How did
this alter Soviet life?

d How does Fainsod explain the changing ideological character of the
Soviet regime under Stalin? How far do you think the changes were
inevitable?

* *e* What do you understand by totalitarianism in the Soviet-Stalinist
sense? In what ways did it differ from Nazism and Fascism?

5 Stalin Reconsidered

The premise of Bolshevism
Their objective was therefore not simply to achieve the revolution in one
particular country, even a country of such gigantic proportions as the
Tsarist empire, spread over two continents. Their objective was world
5 revolution. The revolution which the Bolsheviks accomplished in Russia
was not conceived essentially as a Russian revolution, but as the first step
in a European and world revolution; as an exclusively Russian

phenomenon, it had no significance for them, no validity and no possibility of survival. . . .

10   In this situation, the revolutionary impetus reached the limits of its endurance; NEP represented an inevitable retreat. . . . The great revolutionary goals were laid aside; political programmes gave way to everyday routines, subversive theory to traditional practice. The party was now forced to take on an omnipresent role, not only political but
15 administrative, social and economic. It was thus obliged to swell its ranks, not with agitators or political militants but rather with administrators who could control, manage, manoeuvre and supervise: the men demanded by this new situation.

The genesis of Stalin

20 This was the moment of the greatest cleavage between the vanguard and the class which it ought to have represented. The very results of 1917 seemed on the point of vanishing. With freedom of commerce, NEP introduced measures to facilitate the revival of businessmen, merchants, capitalists. While it benefited the peasantry, more especially rich and
25 middle peasants, it necessarily disappointed the demands of the proletariat which had hitherto had to carry the heaviest burdens of the revolution. The most important element which defined the new situation, already emerging during the NEP period, was the definitive abandonment of the strategy upon which the revolution had been carried out. The last hope of
30 revolution in Europe collapsed. The bourgeois order in Germany, three times on the point of its breakdown, resisted. Its victory both carried within it the seeds of Nazism and contributed to the definitive isolation of the USSR, reinforcing the trend towards retrenchment and post-revolutionary involution.

35   The rise of Stalin to leadership, first within the party and then within the state, must be seen in this perspective. His importance began to emerge with the growing bureaucratization of party and state. But the bureaucracy in its turn developed and expanded because of Russia's extreme backwardness and isolation; it was the product of a revolution in
40 retreat, pinned down within the frontiers of a poverty-stricken economy, dependent on an enormous mass of primitive peasants. . . .

    The failure of the western revolution destroyed the strategy which had hitherto underpinned the practice of the Bolsheviks. The possibility of gradually bridging the gulf between Russian backwardness and a socialist
45 programme, through the industrial and cultural support afforded by the resources of a socialist Europe, was now unpredictably severed. Almost at once the party found itself no longer on solid ground.

    The first result of this new situation was the internal struggle within the Bolshevik leadership after Lenin's death. . . .

50   Isolated and enclosed within the 'Asiatic backwardness' of Russia, the party underwent more than a mere change in strategy. The weight and inertia of the Russian historical legacy now reasserted itself over every force of change and revolutionary rupture. The re-emergent features of the old order were manifested not only in the rebirth of former

ideological and institutional structures, but also . . . in a national restoration. The social forces which now re-emerged from their previous defeat to make their compromise with the new revolutionary order and insensibly to influence its course, were above all forces which re-affirmed the validity of an autochthonous, tradition against foreign influences.

The cause of Russia and the cause of Bolshevism were now fused into an undifferentiated unity. . . . Communism, which had entered Russia with a programme of Westernization (industry, science, modern working class, critical and experimental outlook), condensed in Lenin's formula 'Electrification + Soviets' . . . now began to be impregnated with the corrupt humours of the autocratic Great-Russian mentality. . . .

The consequences of Stalin

. . . Nonetheless this man was in his own way endowed with a 'greatness' that we must in some way attempt to define, more to understand what he produced than what he was himself. The liberal English historian Carr has written: 'Stalin is the most impersonal of the great historical figures.' Through industrialization, 'he Westernized Russia, but through a revolt, partly conscious, partly unconscious against Western influence and authority and a reversion to familiar national attitudes and traditions. The goal to be attained and the methods adopted or proposed to attain it often seemed in flagrant contradiction. . . . Stalin's ambiguous record was an expression of this dilemma. He was an emancipator and a tyrant; a man devoted to a cause, yet a personal dictator; and he consistently displayed a ruthless vigour which issued, on one hand, in extreme boldness and determination and, on the other, in extreme brutality and indifference to human suffering. The key to these ambiguities cannot be found in the man himself. . . . Few great men have been so conspicuously as Stalin the product of the time and place in which they lived.'

It is obvious that this judgement could have no foundation if it were not for the fact that the Stalin period also included industrialization and the great Five Year plans. Through this process Russia became the second industrial power in the world. . . .

> Lucio Colletti, 'The Question of Stalin', *New Left Review*, 61, 1970; reprinted in R. Blackburn, ed., *Revolution and Class Struggle — a reader in Marxist Politics*, Harvester, 1977, pp 164, 177—9, 185—6

Questions

a (i) To what extent was the Bolshevik objective 'world revolution' (lines 4—5)?

    (ii) What was the NEP and in what ways did it represent 'an inevitable retreat' (line 11)? Was its introduction 'the moment of greatest cleavage. . . . to have represented' (lines 20—21)?

    (iii) Explain the meaning and significance of 'The last hope of revolution in Europe collapsed' (lines 29—30).

(iv) In what ways was the bureaucracy of the Stalinist period 'the product of a revolution in retreat' (lines 39–40)?

(v) Why did the party find itself 'no longer on solid ground' (line 47)?

(vi) Show how the forces that emerged in the 1920s in Russia reaffirmed 'the validity of an autochthonous tradition against foreign influences' (lines 59–60)?

b What does Colletti see as the main objective of the Bolsheviks and why did they fail to achieve it in the 1920s and 1930s?

c How does Colletti account for the rise of Stalin?

d How far does Colletti's argument about Stalin's rise to power parallel that of Trotsky (extract 2)?

e 'Stalin is the most impersonal of the great historical figures.' (E. H. Carr) Discuss.

* *f* What were the effects of the successive failures of revolution in Germany?

Further Work

a The origins of Stalinism can be traced to the years before Lenin's death in 1924. Discuss.

b A study of the course of revolution shows that after the initial revolutionary outburst there is a retreat into dictatorship. The Russian experience is no exception. Discuss.

c Soviet writers like to view Stalin as an unfortunate aberration of Soviet history. Do you agree?

d Stalin stands at the end of a long line of Russian autocrats and he was undoubtedly the most efficient. Discuss.

e Why is it so difficult to understand Stalin as a person?

V France – from Victory to Defeat

Introduction

During a discussion on the United States of America, the historian A. L. Rowse ventured the paradox that an apparently democratic country could be so ungovernable. France under the Third Republic was less democratic but equally volatile; David Thomson wrote that its history 'was dominated by the curious rhythm of one supreme crisis every generation – in the five years before 1875, before 1905 and before 1940.' These crises are well known to English historians, but the period between 1919 and 1936 is less familiar. This section concentrates on two themes of the inter-war period, the problems of external and internal security.

As Clemenceau once wryly implied, a combination of traditional Francophobia and geographical security provided by the Channel made Britain unaware of the dangers remaining to France after 1919. The Maginot Line (more properly, the Eastern Fortified Zone) was a necessity, given France's manpower limitations and her frontiers, which were difficult to defend; in reality, it was not the complete solution many Englishmen – and Frenchmen – thought it to be. The French army, ignoring the brilliant exposition of mechanised warfare by a junior officer like de Gaulle, lumbered on, producing good quality *matériel* without understanding how to use it. Comparison with von Seeckt's army (described in extract 2 of section II), which was roughly the same size as de Gaulle's proposed striking force, is chilling.

Internally, France veered from left to right with a bewildering number of ministries: André Maginot served in 26 cabinets between 1920 and 1932. Three left-wing governments fell in similar circumstances during this period, revealing the splits in the political left described by Max Beloff. Opposition to the left from the pro-catholic, pro-fascist 'leagues' reached a climax in the Paris riots of February 1934, an interesting link with the revolutionary *journées* of the nineteenth century.

The collapse in 1940 was a tragic interweaving of the external and internal themes, creating problems for France which were only becoming soluble in the early years of the Fifth French Republic.

Further Reading

D. W. Brogan, *The Development of Modern France 1870–1939*, Hamilton, 1967, a readable collection of essays.

J. P. T. Bury, *France 1814–1940*, Methuen, 1969 edn, and A. Cobban, *A History of Modern France, Vol. III, 1871–1961*, Penguin, 1965; two useful textbooks by well-known historians.

D. Thomson, *Democracy in France since 1870*, Oxford University Press, 1964 edn, a valuable and stimulating thematic study.

D. C. Watt, *Too Serious A Business: European armed forces and the approach to the Second World War*, Temple Smith, 1975, essential reading on the inter-war period for most of the sections of this book.

A. Werth, *France in Ferment*, Jarrolds, 1934, and *The Destiny of France*, Hamilton, 1937; eye-witness accounts of the toils of the Third Republic.

1   The Maginot Line

The role of the army in French politics had always been difficult. It was, as its defenders never ceased to remind the French public, the oldest French institution, much older than the Third Republic, with traditions rooted equally in the armies of the monarchy, the Revolution and the Empire. In

5   essence, it betrayed its divided origin, being an uneasy alliance between the republican idea of the citizen army, the nation in arms, and the tradition of a professional army with an officer class drawn from the hereditary landowners, the catholic nobility. As such it had been through one hundred years or more, since the whiff of grape-shot of Vendémiaire

10   and the expulsion of the deputies on 18th Brumaire, the bulwark of the party of order against the party of movement. It had cleared the streets of Paris in June 1848, suppressed the commune in 1871, and broken in turn the wine-growers in 1907, the Paris general strike of 1908 and the miners of the Nord in 1911–13. Since 1848 it had been regarded as the class

15   weapon of wealth and the social order. . . .

The French army had seen its holy status as the guardian of the national honour and hope of *revanche* broken over the Dreyfus case and its senior officers purged in favour of those whose Freemasonry guaranteed their loyalty to the Republic. Its cherished doctrine, the superiority of the

20   moral over the material and of the attack over the defence, had been obliterated by 1916, together with the flower of its pre-war officer corps. The military mutinies of 1917 had produced a Pétain quiet and long-suffering, in the place of the devotees of Foch and Grandmaison. Foch's return to favour as the Allied Generalissimo had produced military

25   victory at the cost of new and heavy losses, but it was a victory whose effect had been whittled away both at Versailles, and by the failure of the army-sponsored Rhenish separatist movement and Poincaré's invasion of the Ruhr. The financial disasters which followed hit the officer class of the post-war army particularly badly. In 1919–20, much of the surviving

30   elements of *nobilité* and *grande bourgeoisie* among the officer corps had removed themselves by large-scale resignations. The post-war officer class tended to come from the middle and small bourgeoisie and from the

prosperous farming classes, with fixed salaries and capital held in
government bonds. The inflation which defeated Poincaré and brought
35 about the success and subsequent disintegration of the *Cartel des Gauches*
hit those groups particularly badly. The increases in taxation felt
necessary to counter the inflation and the consequent inquisition into
personal finances of the bureaucracy reinforced the hostility of the officer
corps to the parliament, to the Republic and to the former Anglo-
40 American allies 'massed against our finances'. Returns to agriculture fell
badly, ground rents in 1934 being worth barely half of their value in
1914. Officers' wives were forced to take jobs. By the mid-1920s the crisis
of morale in the officer corps, with all chances of promotion blocked by
the top-heaviness of the senior ranks stuffed with wartime appointees,
45 and faced with too many tours of colonial duty in Morocco, Syria or
Indo-China, had reached crisis point. In 1926, Painlevé wrote, 'The
Army is at present the prey of a deep uneasiness. Its *cadres* are dispirited
and look for an opportunity to leave the service. The young turn away
from our military schools.'
50 The atmosphere was made worse by the machinations of the French
parliamentary leaders. Military service had been reduced to eighteen
months in 1923 and in 1928 was cut to one year. The erection of the
Maginot Line became a military necessity when the annual intake was
only just over 100,000 men, due to fall in the 1930s to 70–80,000. . . .

D. C. Watt, *Too Serious a Business: European armed forces and the
approach to the Second World War*, 1975, pp 35–7

55 For the first two years after the end of the First World War, distrust of
Germany was still far too deeply rooted for even the severe terms of the
Treaty of Versailles to bring relief to the fears of France. When these
terms came up before the French Parliament for formal approval the
spokesman for all those who felt they were insufficient for the future
60 safety of the country was ex-Sergeant André Maginot. Dragging an
almost useless leg, supporting himself upon two sticks, he rose to make
prophecies that time would fulfil.

'We are always the invaded, [thundered this wrecked giant of a man from the
tribune] we are always the ones to suffer, we are always the ones to be sacrificed.
65 Fifteen invasions in less than six centuries give us the right to insist upon a
victor's treaty that will offer something more realistic than temporary solutions
and uncertain hopes. They do more; they make it our duty to do so. After all
we have suffered, we have the right to demand certainties. This treaty does not
provide certainties, either in respect of the reparations due to us, or in respect of
70 security. Without proper guarantees of both, it is going beyond the possibilities
of human nature to expect our people to rebuild the regions that remain
exposed to the risks and calamities of a new invasion. . . .'

It was not until the end of 1929, when the 1930 budget came up for
discussion, that Maginot's carefully prepared parliamentary plans could
75 be put into practice. He made no frontal assault. . . .
'We could hardly dream,' he explained, 'of building a kind of Great

Wall of France, which would in any case be far too costly. Instead we have foreseen powerful but flexible means of organising defence, based on the dual principle of taking full advantage of the terrain and of
80 establishing a continuous line of fire everywhere.' He was, he insisted, instituting nothing new, but only carrying on the work of his Left Wing predecessor, Paul Painlevé. He pointed out the absolute need to complete the work by 1935, when the number of young men to be called to the colours each year would fall to its lowest point. . . .

85 The imagination of the public was stirred. In their passionate desire for peace they believed in what they wanted to be true, that France would have an inviolable system of defence protecting her entire eastern and northern frontiers. It was in vain that Maginot, in speeches of the greatest frankness, painted the true picture and repeated again and again that only
90 the north-eastern defences existed, as a measure of security to replace the French occupation of the Rhineland. They would prevent a swift and successful German attack on Alsace and Lorraine; one that, if launched without a formal declaration of war, could not otherwise be resisted. Their extension in the same form to other parts of the frontier was not
95 contemplated.

In a speech in mid-February, 1930, he specifically pointed out that the sole additions to the north-eastern defences then being studied were water-barriers. The proposal was to provide for the flooding of large areas by the use of a system of locks and sluices. This was in fact done later
100 immediately to the west of the major fortifications. Along the northern frontier, he added, it was not easy to take defensive measures, as part of it lay between France and Belgium, and 'it is not possible decently to construct a strong defensive system opposite the territory of this friendly nation'. In this General Weygand, who had been appointed Chief of the
105 General Staff in 1929, concurred. The public paid no attention and went on believing in an impregnable defence of all frontiers to north and east. . . .

The major defensive works were of two types, casemates and *ouvrages*, or fortresses. In general, the line was a succession of casemates; along the
110 Rhine no other form was used. Elsewhere, these casemates were reinforced every 3−5 miles by very powerful fortresses. To these two elements it was considered indispensable from the beginning to add a third one, mobility. Such success as the Germans achieved against the line was due entirely to the weakness or absence of this essential third element.
115 It consisted of Interval Troops, fully equipped with field artillery, which provided continuity of defence, depth of defence and the mobility necessary to throw back enemy attacks. They could be moved forward to defend the approaches to the casemates and relieve the outposts. They could be moved to the rear to protect the weakest part of the fortresses,
120 the entrances. Their artillery could be brought to bear on ground dead to the guns of the forts. Interval troops were to be specially picked men and comprised infantrymen, gunners, sappers and mechanised cavalry units. . . .

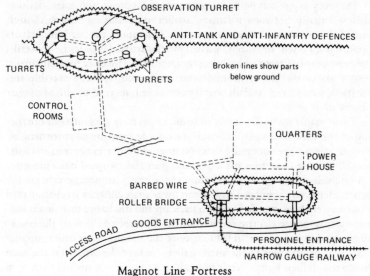

Maginot Line Fortress

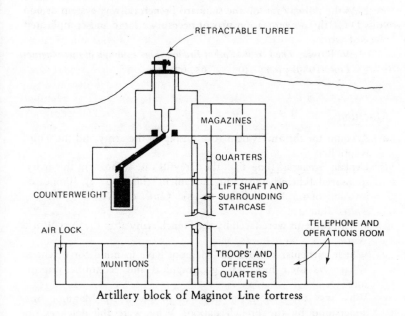

Artillery block of Maginot Line fortress

The fortresses were immense affairs in two parts separated from each other by as much as $1\frac{1}{4}$ miles to obviate one part being put out of action by heavy artillery bombardment of the other, though the more usual distance was from $\frac{1}{4}$ to $\frac{1}{2}$ mile. . . .

The very biggest type had a garrison of 1,000—1,200 men, divided almost equally between infantry, artillerymen and engineers, though
130 with a slight preponderance of gunners. The upper part of both sectors consisted of two or three 'infantry' or 'artillery' blocks, powerful concrete constructions buried deep in the earth. The only parts normally visible above the hill or mound were the turrets, some retractable and rotating, some fixed, and all heavily armoured, serving as gun turrets or
135 observation posts. . . .

These major fortresses were, in some respects, quite fantastic. Emerging at the foot of a steep hill were two wide open mouths formed by openings in a huge concrete block. Neither of these were entrances to the fort, but firing chambers for a 47-mm. gun and twinned machine-guns
140 on one side, twinned machine-guns and a heavy automatic rifle on the other. Between them, and much narrower than either, a steel-shuttered doorway enabled motor trucks to back up and discharge their loads into the narrow-gauge electric railway trucks. In some of the forts the trucks discharged into a powerful lift that took the munitions or other supplies
145 down 75 or 100 feet to the main gallery, where the *Metro* (as the men loved to call their light electric railway) ran to store-rooms and turrets; in others the railway itself descended well-graduated slopes to the lower level. As the railway ran on the standard French railway system of 600 volts D.C., the power station was of necessity a large and complicated
150 piece of work. . . .

V. Rowe, *The Great Wall of France: The Triumph of the Maginot Line*, 1959, pp 17, 49—52, 65, 67—70

Questions

a   Account for the ambivalent relationship of the army and the Third Republic.

b   Explain '*revanche*' (line 17); 'the Dreyfus case' (line 17); 'the army-sponsored Rhenish separatist movement' (lines 26—7); 'Poincaré's invasion of the Ruhr' (lines 27—8); '*Cartel des Gauches*' (line 35); '*cadres*' (line 47).

c   What problems were faced by the French army after the First World War?

* d   Which particular regions did Maginot have in mind for defences? What was their historical, geographical and economic importance?

e   Why was the system of defences proposed by Maginot misunderstood by the French nation? Why were the defences not extended to cover other parts of the frontier?

* f   Discuss the merits of static frontier defences in the light of military developments in Europe between the wars (see the following extract). How did the Maginot Line fortresses fare during 1940?

2 Mechanised Warfare

In the five hours' flight by the Berlin–Paris air route, the traveller sees, marked out on the soil, the safeguards of Germany and the weaknesses of France. On leaving the banks of the Spree he can, during his long enforced leisure over two-hundred-and-fifty miles as far as the Meuse,
5   pick out the moats in the shape of the Elbe, the Aller, the Leine, the Weser, and the Rhine, which protect the capital of the German State far and near; he can contemplate the fortresses of the Harz, Hessian, Rothhaar, and Eifel mountains with which nature has endowed the Germans. Suddenly the land flattens out, grows gentler and more human.
10 There are no longer any mountains or gorges or precipices. We have arrived in France! Hardly is the frontier crossed than this basin-shaped territory which dips towards its centre, those converging rivers, railways and roads, this suburban aspect which the country assumes so rapidly, make one feel that Paris is quite close. And here at once we see the public
15 buildings, warehouses and factories, the focus of a thousand arteries, ill-guarded by low hills, bordered by easily penetrated woods, without any fortifications, a close, coveted and easy prey!

   . . . The policy of a State, said Napoleon, is decided by its geography. France has, through the centuries, sought by diplomacy the protection
20 which nature has denied her. Others have been able to concentrate on the domination of the seas, the exploitation of distant lands and of free outlets, the uniting of a scattered race; but what haunts us most is the safety of our own hexagonal territory. All the schemes prepared and treaties concluded by France during the past thousand years have had as
25 their object the establishment of a political system which should prevent our enemies from molesting us. Thanks to these constantly renewed efforts, we have, indeed, survived, but we are now more than ever bereft of guarantees. . . .

   It is true that at all times France has tried to obscure the breaches in her
30 frontiers by fortifications. She is still doing the same. . . . One cannot value too highly the aid to resistance which permanent works are able to furnish. But these fortifications, quite apart from the fact that they must be given adequate garrisons, are very limited in depth. Besides, they leave the whole of the northern region exposed. And how can one foresee
35 the effects that would be produced on the defenders by modern methods of attack, aircraft, super-heavy tanks and poisonous gases? Moreover, one must take into consideration the possibilities of surrender. For, of all the trials of war, the hardest, on the whole, is reserved for beleaguered troops . . . .
40 A WEAPON FOR REPRESSIVE AND PREVENTIVE ACTION – that is what we have to provide for ourselves. A weapon which can exert from the very outset extreme strength, and can hold the enemy in a state of chronic surprise. The internal combustion engine gives the means of satisfying these conditions of ruthlessness and of

45   suddenness, since it will take whatever is required, where it is needed and with all speed; provided, of course, that it is well handled.

To-morrow the professional army will move entirely on caterpillar wheels. Every element of troops and services will make its way across mountains and valleys on the appropriate vehicles. Not a man, not a gun, not a shell, not a piece of bread, will be transported in any other way. A large formation, striking camp at daybreak, will be a hundred miles away by night. It will need no more than one hour to come from a distance of ten miles, and across any kind of country, and take up its battle position against the enemy, or to disappear, in breaking off contact, out of range of fire and field-glasses. But this speed would be of little value if it could not be reinforced by such power of fire and assault that the rhythm of battle synchronized with that of movement. . . .

Six divisions of the line completely motorized and 'caterpillared', and partly armoured, will constitute an army suitable for carrying through a campaign. It will be an organism whose front, depth and means of protection and supply will allow it to operate independently. Each one of the six larger units will . . . be provided with all that it needs in the way of weapons and supply services to carry on the battle from beginning to end, even if it is encircled by others. . . .

Aerial units intended, not for casual tasks at anyone's behest, but with a definite mission of keeping a single, definite general constantly informed and always supporting the same comrades in battle and lengthening the effective range of familiar artillery, will be the eyes of the main unit. . . .

. . . The most adequate support is . . . that which comes from the air. . . . In order that, at a moment's notice, tanks may be in a position to manoeuvre where they are needed, guns may concentrate their fire on the necessary points, and reserves may be moved up to the right spot, nothing is so useful as the aeroplane which discovers the enemy far off, rapidly signals the position of objectives, and . . . indicates the position of friendly troops. . . . By striking of its own accord on visible targets, the Air Force becomes, *par excellence*, the arm whose lightning effects combine best with the principles of strategic withdrawal and the exploitation of large mechanized formations.

      C. de Gaulle, *The Army of the Future*, 1943 (French edition, 1934), pp 16–19, 33–4, 87–91, 127

Questions

a   Why was France vulnerable to attack from the east?

b   What objections had the author to fixed fortifications?

  *   c   What does de Gaulle recognise as the potential of armoured vehicles? How may his conception of the rôle of aircraft be criticised?

d   Examine the similarities between de Gaulle's motorised army and the German *Blitzkrieg*.

  *   e   Why do you think the author's ideas were not implemented by the

French army Staff? Could his projected army have prevented the fall of France in 1940?

  *   *f* In this book, de Gaulle wrote: '. . . if we were to get possession of the Sarre valley, it would give us 10,000,000 tons of coal a year. Were we to reach the Swabian Danube we would be cutting Austria off from Germany. By debouching on the Main, we would spur the Czechs into action. By seizing Treves and the Eifel plateau we would cover . . . Lorraine, Belgium and Luxemberg. Whoever holds Dusseldorf, paralyses the Ruhr.'

What does this passage suggest about the rôle of this army, and the difficulties faced by French diplomacy and military strategy in the 1930s?

3 Riot or Revolution?

. . . Today, the only thing people seem agreed upon is that [the Paris riots of 6 February 1934] were important. But this importance is looked for in two directions. In the first place, there is the light thrown by the riots on the immediately pre-war phase in the long French tradition of anti-
5 Parliamentary movements of the Right. As a French historian has written recently: 'It is in the perspective of the street riots of the Boulangist movement, of "Panama" and of the Dreyfus case, much more than in that of the march on Rome or the Munich putsch that one should undoubtedly place the "day" of February 6, 1934.' In the second place,
10 the riots are seen as one in a series of events which led to the formation of the Popular Front, in reaction againt the danger, real or alleged, of the setting up of a Right wing dictatorship.

But were the riots themselves part of a deep-laid plot against the Republic? Did the rioters have any clear intentions, or did a political
15 demonstration of a familiar kind get out of hand because of clumsiness or worse on the part of the authorities? . . . In the end France did finish up at Vichy with a non-Parliamentary régime which seemed, both ideologically and in its composition, to fulfil some of the desires attributed to the rioters of the Sixth of February. . . .

20 [After the war Léon Blum commented] 'these same elements, conservative elements for whom the evils of dictatorship counted for little by the side of the benefits of national discipline, and elements of the Left, tempted by the idea of a dictatorial authority applied to the revolution — one finds them joined together and confused on the Sixth of February as at Vichy and under the Vichy
25 régime. . . .

There was a tendency immediately after the "day" of the Sixth of February to make it at one and the same time ridiculous and odious. It was presented as a sort of scuffle, minor but nevertheless bloody, started off by hot-headed youths. . . .

30 This is by no means my opinion. The sixth of February was a redoubtable attempt against the Republic. . . .

I think that there can be no doubt for anyone who was a witness to these events but that the insurrection had within the Chamber itself both representatives and leaders. Their tactics were, I believe, to bring about the fall
35 of the cabinet . . . and to ask the Chamber to disperse. . . . a provisional government would have been proclaimed. . . . I am ignorant . . . as to what the relations of Marshal Pétain may have been with the organisers of the riot. But I believe that his name would have been found on the list of the government. . . .'

40 The Chamber elected in 1932 . . . was incapable . . . of producing a coherent majority because of the fictitious nature of the Left itself. . . . The Socialists were an essential part of any majority of the Left and the Radicals were committed not to rule 'against them'. On the other hand, the Socialists refused out of principle, and because of competition
45 from the Communists on their Left, to participate in the governmental combination, and their support could at any time be withdrawn. Without the Socialists, the Radicals, with whom no possible coalition could arithmetically-speaking dispense, could only govern in harness with elements drawn from the Right. This is a decisive element in a
50 political explanation of the crisis of February 1934.

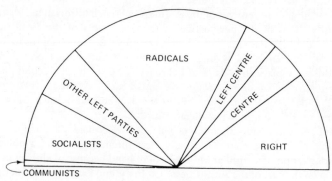

The Chamber of Deputies, 1932

. . . when the 'Stavisky' scandal broke at the beginning of 1934 France was enjoying its fifth ministry in eighteen months. . . . The belief that the career of [Stavisky] had been aided by complicity in the highest circles of the Radical party . . . did provide the movement with an excellent
55 platform for its claim that France's rulers were not merely incompetent but corrupt. . . . In a very real sense the Radical Party was the Republic and the Republic was the Radical Party. . . .

On 6 February, the day on which Daladier was to meet the Chamber, a series of demonstrations was called for by the different Right wing and
60 ex-service groups. . . . One can argue . . . that the dispersal of the meeting-places suggests no collusion. Or one can take the view . . . that

there was some significance in the fact that these meeting places formed something in the nature of a circle with the Chamber of Deputies as its centre. . . .

65 The Chamber . . . met at 3 o'clock and its session was punctuated by violent demonstrations.

Activity on the Place de la Concorde began at about 4 o'clock, when it started filling up both with members of the leagues . . . and with curious onlookers. Mixed with the crowd were a number of Camelots du Roi,
70 the activists of the Action Française, and, so it was later alleged, a number of communists. . . .

By about 5 o'clock . . . young men were demonstrating at the passage of troop-carrying lorries. The mounted Gardes cleared a space on the south side of the Place and a barricade of lorries was put across the
75 bridge. . . .

By about 6 the crowd had become more violent and the police were being pelted with stones, garden chairs, railings . . . charges of this kind took place every few minutes. . . .

At about half-past six the rioters themselves began to build a barricade
80 and were attacked by the police with considerable violence; 22 policemen had to be removed to have their injuries attended to. . . .

At [half-past 7] the column of the Solidarité Française arrived in the Place de la Concorde. . . . They showed every intention of pressing on across the bridge to the Chamber; hoses which were used against them
85 were seized and turned against the police. The rioters got right up to the barricade. . . . The Gardiens de la Paix and the Gardes Mobiles lost their nerve and fired in self-defence . . . 6 rioters were killed and 40 more injured in the firing. . . . The Right wing opponents of the government were later to make a great deal of this firing, their case being that unarmed
90 and patriotic citizens had been brutally shot down. . . . On the other hand, the evidence that the first shots came from the crowd . . . was accepted by the great majority of the Commission. . . .

. . . the disorder inside the Chamber was continuing and some Deputies were slipping away . . . some humorist put outside the door of
95 the Press Gallery the notice 'Avis à les Manifestants – Ici il n'y a pas de Députés'. . . .

At about 8.15 an attempt was made by the police to clear the rioters from a large area. . . . At some time during the next half hour the two groups of Croix de Feu from the north and south of the river joined up to
100 the west of the Chamber and were repulsed by the police outside the Ministry of Foreign Affairs. . . . [At 8.45 the ex-servicemen's procession reached the Place de la Concorde] There were . . . five or six thousand ex-servicemen . . . marching in good order and this for the moment silenced the disturbances. . . .

105 What happened next with regard to the ex-servicemen is one of the disputed points. It is not clear whether they really intended to abandon the demonstration but were prevented from leaving the area by the police . . . or whether . . . they really meant to go to the Élysée to

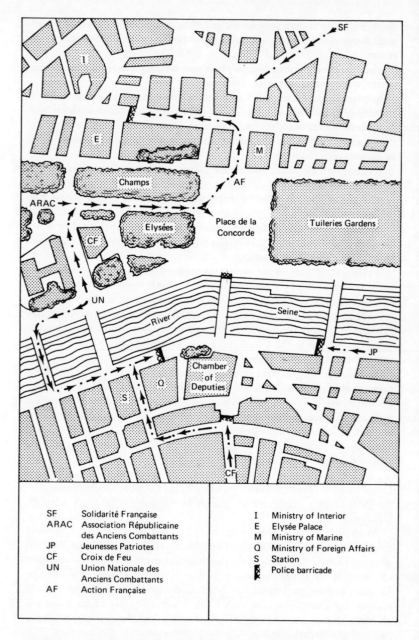

SF	Solidarité Française	I	Ministry of Interior
ARAC	Association Républicaine des Anciens Combattants	E	Elysée Palace
JP	Jeunesses Patriotes	M	Ministry of Marine
CF	Croix de Feu	Q	Ministry of Foreign Affairs
UN	Union Nationale des Anciens Combattants	S	Station
AF	Action Française		Police barricade

present a petition to the President. Anyhow, there was a fairly severe
110 scuffle with the police in the narrow Rue St. Honoré. . . .

At 10 the frustrated ex-servicemen returned to the Concorde in an
ugly mood and proceeded towards the bridge. They got past the first

obstacles and arrived up against the real barricade. The police charged
with batons and used their hoses, and were showered with missiles in
115 return. By 11.30 there had been some fifteen or thirty further mounted
charges by the police, and there were occasional shots from the rioters.
There was a direct attack on the bridge at about 11.30, causing a new
panic among its defenders . . . some of the police fired once more; again,
it seems, spontaneously. . . . Between midnight and 1 o'clock the
120 crowds dispersed and the demonstration came to an end. . . .

The casualities of the evening were later reckoned by the Commission
of Inquiry: On the side of the rioters, 14 killed; 236 taken to hospital and
419 other injured; on the side of the police, 1 killed, 92 taken to hospital
and 688 other injured. . . .

125 The political interest of the period after 6 February does not lie in the
composition or programme of governments but in what was going on in
opposition. On 9 February, the Communists staged a turbulent demonstration of their own; on 12 February, there was a general strike. In face of
the danger, real or imaginery, of a fascist régime in France, and with
130 Soviet policy taking a new line, the foundations of the Popular Front
were gradually and painfully laid. . . .

In conclusion, one must admit that after all there may be no mystery,
that the striking impression made by the map of a planned and purposeful
convergence upon the Parliament buildings may be an illusion, that the
135 rioters may have had little leadership and no defined plans for the seizure
of power, that the threads that link 6 February 1934 to 10 July 1940 may
be too slender to bear the weight of any theory that would seek directly to
connect them. Perhaps there is nothing to it but the familiar story of a
political crisis in Republican France with a little intervention this time by
140 the mob. To the charge of 'attempted murder of the Republic' made by
Léon Blum the only reasonable verdict may be the Scottish one: 'Not
proven'.

M. Beloff, 'The Sixth of February' in James Joll (ed.) *The Decline
of the Third Republic* (St. Antony's Papers No. 5), 1959, pp 9 – 11,
14 – 15, 17 – 18, 22 – 8, 30, 35

Questions

a (i) Briefly identify 'the Boulangist movement', 'Panama' and 'the
Dreyfus case' (lines 6 – 7), and explain their importance in the
history of the Third Republic.

(ii) Who were 'Léon Blum' (line 20); 'Marshal Pétain' (line 37) and
'Daladier' (line 58)?

(iii) What were 'Vichy' (line 17); 'Action Française' (line 70);
'Camelots du Roi' (line 69); 'Solidarité Française' (line 82);
'Croix de Feu' (line 99) and 'the Popular Front' (line 130)?

b What are the opposing views on the riots of 6 February 1934? How
does 'Vichy' fit into the debate?

c What questions would an historian ask of Blum's evidence (lines 20–

39)? Having established the questions, examine critically what Blum
said.

d What part in the political troubles of February 1934 was played by the
Stavisky affair?

e Does the account of the street demonstrations suggest a *coup* against
the government?

* f What were the consequences of the *journée* of 6 February?

4 A La Seine!

Le 28 decembre 1933, éclate le scandale des faux Bons de Bayonne qui
allait devenir l'affaire Stawisky.

Le 7 janvier 1934, Garat, député, maire de Bayonne, est arrêté. Le 8,
Stawisky, dont la retraite est découverte près de Chamonix, se tue. Le
5 même jour, Dalimier, ministre des Colonies, qui avait, en 1926, signé des
lettres utilisées par Stawisky, donne sa démission. . . .

M. Daladier formait son gouvernement le 30 janvier 1934, à la fin de la
matinée. Il avait étendu sa combinaison vers le Centre. . . .

J'arrivai a Paris le mardi matin 6 février pour la réunion du groupe
10 radical-socialiste. Daladier avait annoncé qu'il y viendrait. Il s'y présenta
en effet et je lui souhaitai la bienvenue. Les sentiments étaient divers dans
notre assemblée au sujet d'un cabinet que l'on représentait comme s'étant
porté d'abord vers la droite puis, brusquement, vers la gauche. . . . Je
crus bien agir, pour réaliser l'unité, en invitant le groupe, après un court
15 appel de Daladier, à faire confiance au gouvernement pour la défense des
institutions républicaines. Daladier reprit la parole pour exiger une
approbation totale. Je lui demandai alors expressément si le texte que
j'allais soumettre au groupe lui paraissait suffisant et c'est sur son
assentiment formel que je fis voter l'ordre du jour suivant: 'La Chambre
20 fait confiance au gouvernement pour défendre les institutions républicaines et, repoussant toute addition, passe à l'ordre du jour.'

Les nuées d'orage s'amoncelaient de toutes parts. Ce que fut la séance de
la Chambre, M. Laurent Bonnevay l'a écrit avec son impartialité
ordinaire. Dès que le Président du Conseil commença la lecture de sa
25 déclaration, il fut visible que l'obstruction serait acharnée. Elle visait
spécialement le Ministre de l'Intérieur, M. Frot, que les gauches avaient
applaudi a son entrée. Le Président Bouisson veut suspendre la séance.
Daladier garde la tribune avec un calme que j'apprécie. . . . Assuré de ne
pouvoir obtenir le calme de la discussion, Daladier eut raison de rejeter en
30 bloc toutes les interpellations. C'était la bataille en règle. L'opposition
déposait des demandes de scrutin à la tribune sans doute pour faire
attendre la mobilisation annoncée de la rue. Dans le petit jardin de la
Chambre les premières rumeurs parviennent. On voit se détacher, sous les
lumières du soir, la file des gardes à cheval défendant le pont. Des
35 collègues vont aux informations et rapportent des nouvelles assez
tragiques. Des chevaux de la troupe ont été blessés par des manifestants

qui, au bout de leurs cannes, ont fixé des rasoirs. La Chambre s'agite. Son président doit multiplier les suspensions. Je remarque le calme de Léon Blum. Il y eut un moment où la rupture des barrages put faire craindre une invasion de l'Assemblée. Les interventions devenaient de plus en plus violentes. M. le marquis de Tastes se distinguait dans l'invective. 'Qui a donné l'ordre de tirer?' criait-il au Président du Conseil. Certaines agitations me paraissaient traduire une peur secrète. M. Bouisson eut beaucoup de peine à terminer la séance sur un discours de Franklin-Bouillon qui, véhément selon son usage, insultait le gouvernement menacé et le sommait de partir. Le gouvernement obtenait cependant une large majorité: 343 voix contre 237.

La décision appartenait désormais à la rue et non plus à l'Assemblée. Je sortis du Palais-Bourbon avec quelques amis . . . après avoir salué dans un poste de la Chambre, les gardes blessés. Nous gagnons à pied l'esplanade des Invalides. Un jeune homme me reconnaît; il se met à hurler des injures, attroupe une foule généralement très hostile. Sur le haut du pavé, — je veux dire: sur le trottoir, — une petite femme, appartenant, semble-t-il, à ce que l'on dénomme la bonne société, bondit devant moi en me crachant des grossièretés. Je suis frappé d'un coup de pied à la jambe. J'entends crier: 'A la Seine! A la Seine!' Je me sentais humilié à la pensée qu'un maire de Lyon pouvait finir ses jours dans un fleuve autre que le Rhône. J'osai en faire l'observation dans le temps même où j'avais l'honneur d'être brutalisé non par de la canaille populaire, ainsi que l'on dit, mais par des personnes évidemment fort distinguées qui n'étaient là que pour défendre la cause de l'ordre. Un communiste, avec courage, m'aidait à gagner le barrage d'agents qui gardait le ministère des Affaires Etrangères. Un Croix de Feu donna l'ordre à ses camarades d'arrêter l'attaque. Mes collègues se montrèrent admirables de sang-froid et d'affection. Je ne pouvais songer à regagner mon domicile du boulevard. . . .

Le mercredi 7 février devait être marqué par la démission du cabinet Daladier.

E. Herriot, *Jadis II, D'une guerre à l'autre 1914–1936*, Paris, 1952, pp 374–7

Questions

a   (i)   What was 'La Chambre' (line 19)?
    (ii) Explain 'la bataille en règle' (line 30).
    (iii) How did the demonstrators attack the mounted troops?
    (iv) What was paradoxical about Herriot's attackers?

b   What additional problems are presented to the historian by documents in a foreign language?

c   What evidence is there in the extract of Herriot's political leanings?

d   What was the purpose of the meeting of the radical-socialists which Daladier attended?

e Why was Herriot unpopular with the demonstrators? What was the reason for his thoughts about the Seine?

f Account for the political instability of the Third Republic during the inter-war period.

Further Work

a 'The circumstances of the birth of the Third Republic had isolated and put at enmity with it many of the social groups which would normally be expected to support an established system of government. For these the Third Republic lacked legitimacy. Its corruption, its anti-clericalism, its assault on the army at the time of Dreyfus, were irrevocably against it. After 1920 its achievements became even more insupportable.' (D. C. Watt)

Discuss this statement with reference to the view that what happened to France in 1940 was caused as much by internal collapse as by external forces.

b Assess the background, membership and influence of the 'leagues' in France between the wars.

c Using a relief map, examine the vulnerability of France to external aggression after 1919.

d Why did three left-wing governments in France between the wars leave office soon after their accession to power?

VI   Mussolini and Fascism —
The Last of the Caesars

Introduction

'Fascism lacked a common founder,' G. L. Mosse wrote, 'but all over Europe it sprang out of a common set of problems and imposed a common solution to them.' The movements under the generic title of Fascist were firmly rooted in the social and political conditions of Italy, Germany, Spain and Portugal in the inter-war period. The deaths of Franco of Spain and Salazar of Portugal have now removed the last refuges of Fascism in Europe.

Mussolini, a former Socialist, was the epitome of the Fascist movement until his eclipse by Hitler in the early 1930s. The Fascist government in Italy, led by Mussolini (whose career is portrayed by Denis Mack Smith as an astonishing charade), emerged from a real crisis — political, economic and social — which threatened to destroy the fragile and inequitable unity of the country. The successful Fascist party, which achieved a basis of power in 1922, fused together the hatred of Marxism and democracy, the worship of violence and strength, the corporate ideal and the cult of élites.

In foreign affairs, Mussolini was able to parade his imperial dreams. Remembering Italy's humiliating defeat at Adowa in 1896, the 'mutilated victory' of 1919 and his country's reputation as having a large appetite but very bad teeth, Mussolini invaded Abyssinia in 1935. The result, despite misleading Italian propaganda, was a foregone conclusion. Abyssinia was conquered and the League of Nations' collective security disappeared as well. Despite this success, and boasts of the Mediterranean as *Mare Nostrum*, Mussolini had to face both ways, with anxious eyes on the Brenner frontier. His links with Germany — the Rome–Berlin axis of 1936 — were inevitable but disastrous for Italy in the long term: by 1941 Mussolini was bemoaning Italy's fate to Count Ciano, '[Germany's] conquered states will be colonies. The associated states will be confederated provinces of Germany. Among these the most important is Italy. We have to accept these conditions because any attempt to rebel would result in our being reduced from the position of a confederated province to the worse one of a colony. Even if they should ask for Trieste tomorrow, as part of the German Lebensraum we would have to bow our heads.'

Further Reading

F. L. Carsten, *The Rise of Fascism*, Methuen, 1967, a comparative study of European fascist or protofascist parties.

C. J. Lowe and F. Marzari, *Italian Foreign Policy 1870–1940*, Routledge & Kegan Paul, 1975, useful in connecting Fascist foreign policy with that of its predecessors.

A. Lyttelton, *The Seizure of Power: Fascism in Italy 1919–1929*, Weidenfeld & Nicolson, 1973, a detailed and scholarly analysis of Fascism's achievements during the crucial years.

M. Muggeridge, introduction to *Ciano's Diary 1937–1938*, Methuen, 1952, and M. Muggeridge (ed.), *Ciano's Diary 1939–1943*, Heinemann, 1947; very readable insights into the image and reality of Fascist Italy by Mussolini's Foreign Minister and son-in-law.

D. Mack Smith, *Mussolini's Roman Empire*, Longman, 1976, an excellent and highly-readable account of Fascist Italy's foreign and colonial policies by one of the leading scholars of the period.

E. Nolte, *Three Faces of Fascism*, Weidenfeld & Nicolson, 1969 edn, an analytical survey of Fascism, Nazism and Action Française.

E. M. Robertson, *Mussolini as Empire-Builder: Europe and Africa 1932–36*, Macmillan, 1977, a detailed account and discussion of Italian foreign affairs, concentrating on Abyssinia.

E. Wiskemann, *Fascism in Italy: Its Development and Influence*, Macmillan, 1968, a brief but informative introduction to the main aspects.

1   A Column of Fire

28 July – Ravenna

This night the columns proceeded to the destruction of the vast headquarters of the provincial group of the socialist Cooperatives. There was no other possible reply to be made to the attempt made yesterday on
5   the life of Meriano and the assassination of Clearco Montanari. As usual, the action taken by the fascists took people by surprise. The old palace . . . which was the stronghold of the red leagues was totally destroyed. Fascists only undertake operations of this kind for reasons of absolute political necessity. Unfortunately the civil struggle does not employ half
10   measures. We risk our lives every day. No personal interest spurs us on. The final aim is the salvation of our country. We undertook this task in the same spirit as when we demolished the enemy's stores in war-time. The flames from the great burning building rose ominously into the night. The whole town was illuminated by the glare. We had to strike
15   terror into the heart of our enemies. . . .

30 July – Ravenna

I announced to [the chief of police] that I would burn down and destroy the houses of all socialists in Ravenna, if he did not give me within half an hour the means required for sending the fascists elsewhere. It was a
20   dramatic moment. I demanded a whole fleet of lorries. The police officers

completely lost their heads, but after half an hour they told me where I
could find lorries already supplied with petrol. Some of them actually
belonged to the police station. My pretended reason was that I wanted to
get the exasperated fascists out of the town. In reality I was organizing a
25 'column of fire' . . . to extend our reprisals throughout the province.
. . . This journey began yesterday morning, the 29th, at eleven a.m., and
finished on the morning of the 30th. Almost 24 hours of continuous
travelling, during which no-one had a moment's rest nor touched a bite
of food. We went through Rimini, Sant'Arcangelo, Savignano, Cesena,
30 Bertinoro, all the towns and centres in the provinces of Forli and
Ravenna, and destroyed and burnt all the red buildings, the headquarters
of the socialist and communist organizations. It was a terrible night.
Our passage was marked by high columns of fire and smoke. The
whole plain of the Romagna as far as the hills was given over to the re-
35 prisals of the outraged fascists, determined to break for ever the red
terror.

> I. Balbo, *Diario 1922*, Milan, 1932, pp 102−3, 109
> [translation by Mrs A. Grimsdale]

Questions

a What was the reason for the activities of the fascists in this area during
the 28th to the 30th July?

b What apparent connections are there between Balbo's fascists and the
war-time experience of Italian troops?

c Discuss the use by Balbo of the phrase 'absolute political necessity'
(lines 8−9).

d What light does this document throw on the rôle of the police in the
rise of Fascism?

* e To what extent was the 'red terror' (lines 35−6) a myth or reality in
post-war Italy?

* f Analyse the importance of violence to the popularity and success of
Fascism in Italy.

2 The Rise to Power

'A strange crowd forms under the porticoes, gathers in the cafes on the
piazzas.' It is composed of the demobilized ex-officers 'who have sought
and not found employment'; it is 'a compound of repressed hope and
desperation', of forgotten heroes 'convinced that they can harangue a
5 community as they harangued a battalion in the field': of 'public
employees scarcely able to eat compared with whom a peasant, a league
organizer, a trade union secretary is a gentleman, of swarms of brokers,
shopkeepers, and contractors, hit by the slump, who detest with a deadly
hatred the labour and consumers' co-operatives', of 'students and young
10 graduates' with no clients and grandiose ideals, convinced that their

misfortunes were due to the 'sinister plots of senile politicians', of bands of 'incredible adolescents, boys aged from 16 to 19, envenomed by the bad luck which made the war finish too soon . . . because they wished to go and see it, and do great deeds; educated to admire gunpowder and to give
15 blows by 5 years of fighting exalted by adults; pupils of the sensational film, enamoured of every disturbance': and finally of 'bands of ex-revolutionaries who had become war enthusiasts in 1915 and without union ties . . . anxious to recapture a position of command'. This 'crowd' made Fascism into a mass movement, soon swelled by
20 opportunists of all classes who sensed that the tide had turned. In the spring of 1921, the *fascio* of the city [Bologna] had a membership estimated at between 5000 and 8000. . . .

One of the best descriptions of the social composition of the Fascist movement in the larger cities is given by Agostino Lanzillo:

25 . . . the opinion that the Fascist party should become the political instrument of the middle bourgeoisie is founded on the present composition of the Fascist party in the great cities . . . the *fasci* in Milan are composed in the very great majority of employees, small rentiers and lesser and middling professional men. And what is still more important is that the members of similar organizations
30 are, in the majority, men new to political activity. The scant parliamentary education shown in Fascist assemblies, the prevalence of sentiment, the disorder in discussions, are the results of the absolute lack of political experience among the masses gathered together under the Fascist emblem. Fascism is composed in the large cities of new men. They formed the crowd which before the war
35 watched political events with indifference and apathy and which has now entered the contest. Fascism has mobilized its forces from the twilight zones of political life, and from this derives the unruly violence and juvenile exuberance of its conduct. . . .'

The plan for the March on Rome had been drawn up in a secret
40 meeting on 24 October in a Naples hotel. The plan called for the occupation of public buildings throughout north and central Italy as the first stage in the seizure of power; in the second stage three columns would concentrate on the roads leading into Rome, Monterotondo and Tivoli, and converge on the capital. If the Government resisted, the
45 Ministries were to be occupied by force. In reality, the March on Rome, in the strict sense, was a colossal bluff. The city was defended by 12,000 men of the regular army, under the loyal General Pugliese, who would have been able to disperse the Fascist bands without difficulty. Many of the Fascists failed to arrive at their points of concentration; they were
50 travelling by train and were stopped by the simple expedient of taking up a few yards of track. Those who did arrive were poorly armed and they were short of food. They could do nothing except hang around miserably in the torrential autumn rain. The grandiose 'pincer move-ment' on Rome could never have been carried out with any chance of
55 success. . . .

What needs emphasis is that the March on Rome was almost

inconceivably ill-planned if the intention really had been to seize the central State machine by force — when the only way would have lain in a rapid *coup de main*, not in a ponderous concentration. But politically it was
60 essential to avoid surprise. The Government and the King could not be threatened too directly; they must instead be put in a position where they would have to take a positive initiative to restore order. . . . the Fascist action was successful in creating an atmosphere of confusion and an impression of the widespread collapse of State power which during the
65 critical night of 27–8 October could not fail to have a grave psychological effect. For this we have the testimony of Facta's *chef de cabinet*, Efrem Ferraris:

'. . . at the Viminale, the telephones which linked the prefecture to the Ministry gave no respite and after midnight the news became alarming. In the
70 night I witnessed, in the silence of the great rooms of the Viminale, the disintegration of the authority and power of the State. On the large sheets of paper which I kept in front of me, there grew ever thicker the names of the occupied prefectures that I was noting down, the indications of invaded telegraph offices, of military garrisons who had fraternized with the Fascists,
75 providing them with arms, of trains requisitioned by the militia which were directed, loaded with armed men, towards the capital. . . .'

We must now return to Rome, the central government and the King. All that has been said does not, of course, alter the fact that this was the point of decision. At 8 pm on 27 December, when the King arrived in
80 Rome from his country residence of S. Rossore, he told Facta that the Crown must be able to decide in full liberty, and not under the pressure of Fascist rifles. His determination to resist seemed evident. It was not out of character; Victor Emmanuel III had behaved as a correct constitutional monarch, and in 1919 he had courageously resisted Nationalist and anti-
85 parliamentary pressures. To more than one visitor, he had then repeated that he was ready to take a rifle and go down into the piazza in order to defend parliament against a hypothetical military coup. But by October 1922 everything looked very different. The long and painful parliamentary crises had had their effect; in the last stages of the par-
90 liamentary crisis of July the King had scarcely concealed his impatience at the protracted failure to find any effective government. . . .

The explanations which Victor Emmanuel gave of his refusal to sign the emergency decree in 1945 are vitiated by their purpose as Royalist propaganda: and all his retrospective statements, indeed, are marked by a
95 desire to put his decision in the best light possible, according to the different dates when they were offered. The excuse that he quite literally ceded to *force majeure*, convinced that the garrison of Rome was too small and too unreliable to resist the Fascist attack, will not hold. However some part of these several statements may be helpful in understanding the
100 King's state of mind: 'At difficult moments everyone is capable of indecision . . . few or none of those who can take clear decisions and assume grave responsibilities. In 1922 I had to call "these people" to the

Government because all the others in one way or another, had abandoned
me'; on other occasions the King spoke of his desire to 'avoid bloodshed
105 given the news from the provinces which were already in the hands of the
Fascists', and said that if he had acted otherwise, 'it would have been civil
war'. Both these elements in his apologies do seem to correspond to what
we know of his feelings and of the actual situation in 1922; . . .

It seems plain that the King's decision must have looked greater and
110 more serious at the end of the night than at the beginning. If the
Government counter-measures had been immediately effective, if the
occupations had been prevented or the leaders of the movement arrested,
the proclamation of martial law might have resolved the situation
without a general conflict: by the morning this had become much more
115 doubtful.

By themselves, these considerations might not, however, have been
enough to make the King give way. Probably if he had been sure of the
loyalty of the Army, he would have given orders for the troops to re-
establish order. . . .

120 But when all objective elements, the indecisiveness of the government,
the partial success of Fascist tactics, the open collusion of some
generals, . . . the fear of the Duke of Aosta, have been added up, there
remains a margin of doubt which must be ascribed to the character of
Victor Emmanuel. By temperament he was a pessimist, and he had little
125 confidence in either his advisers or his subjects. He was keenly conscious
that, more intelligent than the general run of monarchs, he did not have
the presence or the warmth to inspire personal devotion. Finally his
sceptical nature doubted, not altogether wrongly, the solidity of the
Kingdom of Italy; the old lands of the Crown of Savoy were one thing,
130 but not all Italians were Piedmontese or Sardinian. All authority depends
on confidence; and the King, rational to a fault and with a low opinion of
man in general, had none. He gave way, one can suggest, because to him
the evidence of his solitude had become overwhelming: the only man
who could do anything was convinced of his impotence.

A. Lyttelton, *The Seizure of Power: Fascism in Italy 1919–1929*,
1973, pp 61, 67, 85–7, 89–91, 93

Questions

a   Define 'rentiers' (line 28); 'the March on Rome' (line 45). Identify
    'Facta' (line 80); 'the Duke of Aosta' (line 122).
b   What were the effects of the aftermath of the First World War on the
    growth of Fascism?
c   Which social groups supported the Fascist party?
d   Why was 'the March on Rome' a myth? What importance did the
    Fascists attach to it?
e   What role did Victor Emmanuel III play in the 1922 crisis?
* f   Are there similarities between Hitler's rise to power in Germany (see
    section VII) and Mussolini's in Italy?

3 Mussolini Speaks

Being anti-individualistic, the Fascist system of life stresses the importance of the State and recognises the individual only in so far as his interests
coincide with those of the State, which stands for the consciousness and
universality of man as an historic entity. It is opposed to classic
5 Liberalism . . . Liberalism denied the State in the name of the individual;
Fascism reasserts the rights of the State as expressing the real essence of the
individual. And if liberty is to be the attribute of living men and not that
of abstract dummies invented by individualistic Liberalism, then Fascism
stands for liberty and for the only liberty worth having, the liberty of the
10 State and of the individual within the State. The Fascist conception of the
State is all-embracing; outside it no human or spiritual values may exist,
much less have any value. Thus understood Fascism is totalitarian and the
Fascist state, as a synthesis and a unit which includes all values, inter-
prets, develops and lends additional power to the whole life of the
15 people.
   A nation, as expressed in the State, is a living, ethical entity only in so
far as it is progressive. Inactivity means death. Therefore the State does
not only stand for Authority which governs and confers legal form and
spiritual value on individual wills, but it is also Power which makes its
20 will felt and respected beyond its own boundaries, thus affording
practical evidence of the universal character of the decisions necessary to
ensure its development. This implies organisation and expansion,
potential if not actual. . . .
   Fascism, in short, is not only a lawgiver and a founder of institutions,
25 but is an educator and a promoter of spiritual life. It does not merely aim
at remoulding the forms of life, but also their content, man, his character
and his faith. To achieve this purpose it enforces discipline and makes use
of authority, entering into the mind and ruling with undisputed sway.
Therefore it has chosen as its emblem the Lictor's rods, the symbol of
30 unity, strength and justice. . . .
             B. Mussolini, *La dottrina del fascismo*, Rome, 1941

It is, therefore, necessary to be prepared for war not to-morrow but today. We are becoming – and shall become so increasingly because this is
our desire – a military nation. A militaristic nation I will add, since we are
not afraid of words. To complete the picture, warlike – that is to say,
35 endowed ever to a higher degree with the virtues of obedience, sacrifice,
and dedication to country. This means that the whole life of the nation,
political, economic, and spiritual, must be systematically directed
towards our military requirements. War has been described as the Court
of Appeal, but pursue the course dictated by their strength and by their
40 historical dynamic nature, it falls that, in spite of all conferences, all
protocols, and all the more or less highest and good intentions, the hard
fact of war may be anticipated to accompany human kind in the
centuries to come just as it stands on record at the dawn of human
history.

Extract from speech by Mussolini to the General Staff, *The Times*,
28 August 1934, quoted in C. J. Lowe and F. Marzari, *Italian
Foreign Policy 1870–1940*, 1975, p 400

45 . . . All knots were cut by our gleaming sword, and the African victory
remains in the history of the fatherland entire and unsullied, a victory
such as the legionaries that have fallen and those that survive dreamed of
and willed. Italy has her empire at last: a fascist empire because it bears the
indestructible tokens of the will and of the power of the Roman lictors,
50 because this is the goal towards which, during fourteen years, were
spurred on the exuberant and disciplined energies of the young and
dashing generations of Italy. An empire of peace, because Italy desires
peace, for herself and for all men, and she decides upon war only when it
is forced upon her by imperious, irrepressible necessities of life. An
55 empire of civilization and of humanity for all the populations of
Abyssinia. That is in the tradition of Rome, who, after victory, associated
the peoples with their own destiny.

Speech by Mussolini, 9 May 1936, from *Corriere della Sera*, 10
May 1936, quoted in Lowe and Marzari, *op. cit.*, p 406

Questions

a In what ways does Fascism differ from 'classic Liberalism' (line 5)?
b What aspects of Fascist foreign policy are latent in the first document?
c Why can war be described as 'the Court of Appeal' (lines 38–9)?
d What is the evidence that Mussolini saw himself as heir to the Caesars?
* e Why was Abyssinia considered important to the Fascists? What
      methods were used to conquer it?
* f To what extent was Fascist foreign policy influenced by the
      'mutilated victory' of 1919?

4 Mussolini – a Tragi-Comic Leader?

Mussolini more than once proclaimed that war was the ultimate test by
which a nation and a leader should be judged, and obviously by this self-
imposed measurement he was a failure. The style of life which in twenty
years of government he held up for admiration was essentially a military
5 one, and he himself after 1930 seldom appeared out of uniform, yet he
never provided the real sinews of war which his policy required. . . .

'Words', he once remarked, 'are beautiful things, but muskets,
machine guns, ships, planes, and cannon are still more beautiful'; . . .

In public he repeated that 'war is to man what maternity is to woman',
10 it is the normal condition in which men have to live and should be
welcomed even at the risk of destroying civilisation itself. . . .

These remarks came from someone who was not only Prime Minister
but also the minister who simultaneously took responsibility for all three
armed services. In addition he had military as well as political command,

15 for Mussolini held the highest rank of all as First Marshal of the Empire, apart from being commander of the fascist militia, and in 1940 he appointed himself Commander-in-Chief of all the armed forces on all fronts, which left him responsible for just about everything. Such pluralism was the most obvious reason why none of his jobs was properly
20 done. Without doubt some of the most important areas of military provision escaped his eye altogether, since he was never seen in some of the departments of which he was titular head, and on the same day could sign contradictory decrees in several of the eight ministries where administration was kept in his own hand. . . .

25 Mussolini's one undisputed skill was as a propagandist, and ironically it was his success in this field which turned out to be Italy's undoing. All his life he was a professional journalist and even as Prime Minister continued to earn a considerable income by writing. He used to say that Italians read no more than headlines in newspapers, and he therefore especially prided
30 himself on his ability to coin headlines and decide their size and layout. But there came a point where journalism merged into, and corrupted, politics. When he thought up the phrase about 'eight million bayonets', or 'darkening the sky with his aircraft', these were at first figures of speech, but gradually they seem to have taken the place of reality in his
35 own mind. Some people noted a connection here with the current idealist philosophy of Giovanni Gentile which Mussolini accepted for a time as the unofficial doctrine of his regime; if the external world does not exist objectively but is the creation of will or spirit, it might be sufficient to will strongly, to want something, and it would be true. . . .

40 Prestige and propaganda were two of the most important words in Italian fascism. They help to explain Mussolini's yearning for military victory as the most desirable of all achievements. In 1931 he suddenly ordered preparation for an invasion of southern France, and when dissuaded from this by his generals he instead put up the idea of a surprise
45 attack of Jugoslavia by fifty battalions of blackshirts on bicycles. . . .

The General Staff was preparing for the Ethiopian war at least as early as 1932, long before the incident took place at Wal Wal which later became the official excuse for beginning hostilities. Once the Italian invasion had begun in 1935, Mussolini insisted on directing the war from
50 thousands of miles away, and used to shower orders on the local field commanders, sometimes as many as a hundred telegrams a day. These orders reveal a somewhat amateurish idea of strategy, though his energy and drive were quite remarkable, and he can personally claim much of the credit for victory. Unfortunately he deluded himself thereby into
55 overestimating Italy's strength and also into thinking that he had a special instinct for military matters. To impress his people he invented the myth that foreign experts had believed that Italy would be defeated by Ethiopia, and so doing, by announcing that he had won in defiance of all expectations, he dangerously increased popular illusions about his own
60 military capacity. . . .

The Ethiopian war also gave Mussolini a strange feeling of infallibilty.

In private he spoke of forming a black army with which to dominate the whole African continent, and there was wild talk of a million native troops and, even more improbably, of setting up heavy industry in East Africa to produce armaments on a grand scale. Some of his colleagues were perplexed when he began coupling his own name with that of Napoleon. . . .

In August 1936 Mussolini surprised the experts by announcing that he could mobilise eight million men 'in a few hours, by a simple order'. Where he dug up this figure it is hard to say. In a typically fascist manner the eight million eventually became ten or even twelve million, because the whole point of propaganda was that it should sound impressive. . . .

By another interesting piece of legerdemain the composition of army divisions was reduced to two regiments instead of three. This impressively increased the number of divisions by a stroke, but Mussolini subsequently forgot what he had done and hence miscalculated the strength of his army at a crucial stage of the Second World War. The military establishment welcomed the change because more divisions meant more divisional generals, so much so that Farinacci was soon complaining the army looked like a Mexican army. The number of senior officers had to be kept secret after 1938 for fear of ridicule, and Luigi Federzoni was informed that there were more generals than subalterns. . . .

The first real proof that there was a gaping void behind . . . fascist claims arose out of the Italian occupation of Albania in April 1939. The official story was that this example of a lightning war showed the perfection of Italian military organisation, but in fact almost everything went wrong that could have possibly gone wrong. Far from being able to turn the British out of the Mediterranean, the comment made by the permanent secretary of the Italian Foreign Office was that if only the Albanians had possessed an effective fire brigade they would have thrown the invaders back into the Adriatic. Mussolini allowed himself some momentary doubts, but everyone busily covered up the disaster and a few weeks later he was planning to invade Jugoslavia and Greece. Even his Foreign Minister, Galeazzo Ciano, began to be worried that fascism might be losing touch with reality. . . .

The Duce had specified that his doctrine of a lightning war made it necessary to motorise the whole nation. For the public record he also boasted of possessing three armoured divisions, and propaganda put out that these divisions had some 25-ton tanks and equipment which was the most advanced anywhere; but foreign observers knew perfectly well that, apart from a few experimental prototypes, there was nothing bigger than four-ton armoured cars which had been copied from a similar British vehicle and which had proved a dangerous liability in Spain. These armoured cars were splendidly fast, but they carried nothing bigger than machine guns; they could be penetrated by small-arms fire; they had no radio and almost no vision, and according to the Commander of one 'armoured division' they preferably had to be guided by infantry walking

ahead. Nevertheless, knowing that they were almost worse than useless,
110 production continued. Italians had been handicapped in this field by the
fact that they had not used tanks in 1915–18. General Caracciolo, who
was in charge of technical services, took drawings to Mussolini for several
types of possible medium tank, and after listening to him Mussolini
pointed to one drawing and said 'make this one'. Hundreds of millions of
115 lire were thus committed by a complete amateur who trusted his own
intuition, but the system was such that no one else could have taken such a
decision. When the first of the new machines began to come off the line,
they were already out of date and the army recommended stopping
manufacture, though they went on being produced throughout the war
120 simply because there was nothing else available. . . .

. . . above all the explanation of Italy's weaknesses must be sought in
his great sense of showmanship and in the propaganda–consciousness
which allowed him to seize on the dangerous half-truth that it was less
important to do things in politics than to seem to do things, . . .

125 Of course there continued to be considerable difference between public
and private statements. The public version was that Italy had twelve
million men ready to fight, whereas in fact only one and a quarter million
were called up; nor were there even enough trousers for this reduced
number, and Marshal De Bono found many in their underpants. . . .
130 Mussolini once described his technique thus:

> . . . one must try hard not to disillusion people. You must always be doing
> things and obviously succeeding. The hard part is to keep people always at their
> window because of the spectacle you put on for them. And you must do this for
> years. Now I have succeeded in never boring the Italians; I have kept them
135 > tensed up in a state of exaltation by always offering them something new.

This was his great skill. But he knew that it was a dangerous game. You
had to go on building up the stakes in order to make today's spectacle
more splendid and dramatic than yesterday's. Once you failed in this, the
game was over, for people stopped being excited and hence ceased to
140 believe. . . .

This was a world where you could fool most of the people fairly easily,
where decisions could be reversed from day to day without anyone
noticing, and where in any case decisions were designed to impress rather
than to be put into effect. It was an unserious world, where prestige,
145 propaganda and public statements were the things that counted; and it is
hard to avoid the conclusion that this was the central message and the real
soft core at the heart of Italian fascism. . . .

D. Mack Smith, *Mussolini as a Military Leader*, Stenton Lecture
1973, University of Reading, 1974, pp 1 *ff*

Questions

a   What were Mussolini's particular skills? Was he aware of them?
b   'The "dynamic" of Fascism was only finally broken when the

hollowness of Mussolini's military pretensions was revealed.'
(A. Lyttelton) What examples are given of this, and how did
Mussolini attempt to conceal his military problems?
* *c* Was subservience to the Duce a necessary component of Fascism?
  d Mussolini once said, 'Illusion is perhaps the only reality in life.' Was
     this true of Fascist Italy?
* *e* Do you think Smith goes too far in his portrayal of Mussolini?
* *f* Was Mussolini an opportunist? If so, where can this be recognised?

Further Work

a 'The origin of the Right lies always in the challenge of the Left.'
   (E. Nolte)
   'The most convincing proof that Fascism was essentially and literally a
   reaction can be seen in the fact that before 1922 it took root only in
   those areas of Italy where there was a strong Socialist party.'
   (A. Lyttelton)
   Discuss these statements on the growth of Fascism in Italy.
b Had Fascism a greater intellectual foundation than Nazism?
c How realistic was Mussolini's foreign policy? What is revealed in his
   comment of 4 February 1939 that Italy was a prisoner in the
   Mediterranean: 'The bars of this prison are Corsica, Tunisia, Malta
   and Cyprus – its sentinels are Gibraltar and Suez.'?
d 'December 1, 1941 . . . I have protested . . . about the publication . . . of some photographs showing that our prisoners in Egypt
   are having a great time – football, concerts, gaiety. Mussolini is
   concerned about it. "It is a known fact," he says, "that they are
   inclined to let themselves be taken prisoners. If they see that their
   comrades are having such a good time over there, who can hold them
   back?" . . .
      March 7, 1942 The Duce, who is dissatisfied with the way things
   are going, said: "This war is not for the Italian people. The Italian
   people are not mature or consistent enough for so grave and decisive a
   test. This war is for the Germans and the Japanese, not for us."'
      M. Muggeridge (ed.), *Ciano's Diary 1939–1943*, 1947, pp 404,
      443

   Consider whether these extracts, used in conjunction with others in
   this section, suggest a genuine flaw in the Italian people which would
   make them unsuitable for Fascism or war.

VII Nazism – A Problem of Perception

Introduction

One of the challenges facing historians is the ability to empathise, to be able to understand the point of view of people in different contexts of time and place who believed that their ideas and actions were right. In a democracy the student of Nazism has this problem. How could rational Germans support a vicious, racialist, totalitarian group like the NSDAP? Was it credible that 'ordinary' Germans experienced the charisma of Hitler as did Goebbels: 'The man [Hitler] . . . looked at me for a moment. His blue eyes met my glance like a flame. This was a command. At that moment I was reborn. . . . Now I know which road to take.'?

Even in power the aims of the National Socialist movement were only evident after several years, by which time totalitarian control had been achieved. Expansion and conflict lay at the heart of the party's beliefs; as Alan Milward wrote, 'The impact of fascism on other European states was certainly as important as that of jacobinism in 1792 or bolshevism in 1917. Ultimate safety for the National Socialist revolution lay in a reorganization of Europe, the New Order.'

Most of the documents in this section are by eyewitnesses in the Germany experiencing the death-throes of the short-lived Weimar Republic or the increasing hold over all aspects of life by the Nazi machine. They reveal fear, despair and hope: fear at the growth of the Left, fear of the consequences of economic depression, fear of the Jews, despair at the inability of the Weimar governments to bring the economic or political problems (especially those of the treaties of 1919) under control, and hope in the person of Adolf Hitler and in the conservatism of the army.

The role of propaganda in the success of the Nazi party once in power can best be appreciated by viewing newsreels (as in the Historical Association/Macmillan compilation, *The 1930s: Nazi Germany*, 1976) or Riefenstahl's *The Triumph of the Will*, where Henderson's graphic description of the Nuremberg rallies is compellingly portrayed. Few were able, or willing, to look behind the façade of Nazism to see its inner corruption. As W. S. Allen wrote of Thalburg, 'Hardly anyone . . . grasped what was happening. There was no real comprehension of what the town would experience if Hitler came to power, no real understanding of what Nazism was.' Here lies the challenge to the student of Nazism.

Further Reading

K. D. Bracher, *The German Dictatorship*, Weidenfeld & Nicolson, 1974, a lucid and scholarly analysis of the causes and course of National Socialism in Germany.

A. Bullock, *Hitler: A Study in Tyranny*, 1952, Penguin edn 1962, a classic biography, even if becoming dated.

J. Fest, *Hitler*, Weidenfeld & Nicolson, 1974, a good modern biography, particularly valuable on the rise of Hitler.

R. Grunberger, *A Social History of the Third Reich*, Weidenfeld & Nicolson, 1971, a multi-faceted book with plenty of good, interesting examples to dip into.

J. Noakes and G. Pridham (eds.), *Documents on Nazism, 1919–1945*. Cape, 1974, a comprehensive selection of documents on many facets of Nazism, with good introductory and intermediate comments.

A. Speer, *Inside the Third Reich*, Weidenfeld & Nicolson, 1971, a view from within by Hitler's architect.

J. P. Stern, *Hitler: the Führer and the People*, Fontana, 1975, another valuable modern survey, especially on Hitler's political ideology.

1 Personal Encounter

There were many, however, among one's friends and acquaintances, decent people of good family and upbringing, who for the moment were ready to give their support to the new government. It must be remembered that in the course of the fifteen years which separated that
5 day from the Armistice of 1918, Germany had experienced governments of every kind of political combination and complexion, had suffered a terrifying national bankruptcy, had failed to obtain any major measure of treaty revision that was not already *de facto* and who genuinely believed that economic breakdown, a paralysing inflation and a Communist *Putsch*
10 were both possible, probable and imminent. On these fears and memories Hitler had based his popular appeal. He had something for everyone in his bag of promises, and above all he offered an attractive – almost a romantic – prospect for youth. Where Brüning had called for sacrifices and had gained no concessions in return, Hitler offered pledges and made
15 no concessions.

I offer these facts not in any way as an excuse for my friends' action but as an explanation. 'He's our last chance,' I heard over and over again in their houses when speaking of Hitler. 'We've got to let him have his opportunity. After all the Nazis are a minority in the government; the
20 Old Man and 'Fränzchen' are sound at heart, and, if the worst comes to the worst, the Army can always turn the Nazis out.' It became a self-hypnotic chant which blinded and deafened many to what followed. The

tragedy was that in their last argument they were right. The Army could have disposed of Hitler and the whole Nazi gang at any time during the next four years if they had had the leadership and the intestinal fortitude to do so. . . .

It was not long before the Brown Terror, in the form of domestic espionage, began to infiltrate the lives of everyone. At first it was pretty amateurish. 'Bugging' – now a household word – was still in its comparative infancy forty years ago, and when one made a call from a telephone box one was aware of a pause and then a click as the monitoring record was turned on. This technique soon improved, however, and one dreaded the appearance of a telephone maintenance man who would suddenly arrive to rectify a fault which had never been reported. From then on it was assumed that a microphone had been inserted in the instrument not to record talks made on the telephone itself but conversation in the room in which the telephone was. It was not long before some inventive character discovered that a large tea-cosy placed over the telephone rendered it 'safe' and there was an immediate run on tea-cosies, but the enemy soon counter-attacked. The unwelcome visitor would now be an electrician to see about a short-circuit or some other defect in the lamps in several rooms, and once again the pall of uncertainty and fear would paralyse social life.

The technique of conducting a successful system of terror is to terrorise the maximum number of people with the minimum amount of effort. It is manifestly impossible to listen in to every telephone call or to overhear every conversation, but the art lies in the use of the spot-check, thereby letting people know when they were *not* being monitored. This itself was unnerving, but so was the increase in the spying by servants on their employers – and even *vice versa*. One closed the door carefully and conducted conversations in a whisper. One looked over one's shoulder in a public place before speaking. One did not trust the mails. One chose with great care the rendezvous where one met one's friends. No one who has not experienced it can imagine the frighteningly oppressive atmosphere of a totalitarian regime. . . .

I never came under the personal spell of Hitler, but one cannot deny the almost mesmeric magnetism which he did exercise on others – both individually and in the mass. A great meeting in the Sportpalast, of which I attended several, was a spectacle never to be forgotten. Theatrical production at public assemblies of this kind was a strong point with the Nazis and they understood the technique of it very well. The Hall was always packed with men and women and youngsters, mostly in Party uniform, long before the advertised hour. Brass bands would play the *Horst Wessel Lied* and other Party songs and, thus accompanied, the audience would sing at the tops of their voices. 'Warming-up' speeches would be made by Party orators to create an atmosphere of excitement, and then suddenly the hall would be plunged in darkness except for one spotlight focused on Hitler as he made his way to the platform. He was greeted with cheers, of course, but the effect of his speech, whatever its

70 subject – and it rarely varied except in detail – produced such fanatical enthusiasm as I have never seen elsewhere. That terrifying repetition of 'Sieg Heil' and 'Ein Volk, ein Reich, ein Führer' still haunt me and the idolisation reflected in the faces of the listeners, especially the young men and girls, was both poignant and frightening. There is no doubt that for
75 twelve years Hitler held the souls of the majority of the German people under an evil and shameful spell. . . . It was in the safety of Switzerland that I read of the horrors of the Night of the Long Knives, the massacre of 30 June 1934. . . .

How closely I myself escaped I only learned a little later. There had
80 been in the receptionists' office at the Kaiserhof a young Englishman who was learning the hotel business and was doing his year's apprenticeship in Germany at this hotel. We had spoken occasionally and when I next went to Paris some time in July I found him doing his 'French year' at the Crillon. He asked to take me up to my room and there told me that on the
85 morning of 30 June, the S.S. and Gestapo had ransacked and wrecked my rooms at the Kaiserhof and had been furious that I had escaped them. 'I hope,' he said, 'that you are not planning to return to Germany.'

Later still I asked a German friend of mine, who had left the Reich for good but had held an official position which enabled him to have seen my
90 Gestapo file, what would have happened to me. After all, I said, I was a foreigner and not unknown in Berlin, or, for the matter of that, in London. 'Oh,' he said, 'they intended to kill you all right. They had recordings of all your talks with Papen. Then they'd have shot the boys who shot you. All an unfortunate mistake, you know. It would have been
95 too easy.' . . .

J. Wheeler-Bennett, *Knaves, Fools and Heroes in Europe between the Wars*, 1974, pp 68–70, 73, 77–8, 92

Questions

a What does the author think was Hitler's appeal to 'decent people' (line 2)?

b Are there any insights into the success of the Nazis over other parties?

c To what extent is propaganda seen as important to the Nazis?

d Writing 40 years after many of these events, how reliable do you think the author is likely to be?

e Could the Nazi party have achieved so much without the leadership of Hitler? What were his qualities as a leader?

* f What echoes and visions of imperial Germany still influenced the people of Germany during the inter-war years?

2 Party Meetings

How hard it is to upset emotional prejudices, moods, sentiments, etc., and to replace them by others, on how many scarcely calculable influences and conditions success depends, the sensitive speaker can judge by the fact that even the time of day in which the lecture takes place can have a decisive influence on the effect. The same lecture, the same speaker, the same theme, have an entirely different effect at ten o'clock in the morning, at three o'clock in the afternoon, or at night. I myself as a beginner organised meetings for the morning, and especially remember a rally which we held in the Munich Kindl-Keller as a protest 'against the oppression of German territories'. At that time it was Munich's largest hall and it seemed a very great venture. In order to make attendance particularly easy for the adherents of the movement and all others who came, I set the meeting for a Sunday morning at ten o'clock. The result was depressing, yet at the same time extremely instructive; no one became warm, and I myself as a speaker felt profoundly unhappy at being unable to create any bond, not even the slightest contact, between myself and my audience. I thought I had not spoken worse than usual; but the effect seemed to be practically nil. Utterly dissatisfied, though richer by one experience, I left the meeting. . . .

This should surprise no one. Go to a theatre performance and witness a play at three o'clock in the afternoon and the same play with the same actors at eight at night, and you will be amazed at the difference in effect and impression. A man with fine feelings and the power to achieve clarity with regard to this mood will be able to establish at once that the impression made by the performance at three in the afternoon is not as great as that made in the evening. The same applies to a movie. This is important because in the theatre it might be said that perhaps the actor does not take as much pains in the afternoon as at night. But a film is no different in the afternoon than at nine in the evening. No, the *time* itself exerts a definite effect, just as the hall does on me. There are halls which leave people cold for reasons that are hard to discern, but which somehow oppose the most violent resistance to any creation of mood. Traditional memories and ideas that are present in a man can also decisively determine an impression. . . .

In all these cases we have had to do with an encroachment upon man's freedom of will. This applies most, of course, to meetings attended by people with a contrary attitude of will, who must now be won over to a new will. In the morning and even during the day people's will power seems to struggle with the greatest energy against an attempt to force upon them a strange will and a strange opinion. At night, however, they succumb more easily to the dominating force of a stronger will. For, in truth, every such meeting represents a wrestling bout between two opposing forces. The superior oratorical art of a dominating preacher will succeed more easily in winning to the new will people who have themselves experienced a weakening of their force of resistance in the most natural way than those who are still in full possession of their mental tension and will. . . .

In this wrestling bout of the speaker with the adversaries he wants to convert, he will gradually achieve that wonderful sensitivity to the psychological requirements of propaganda, which the writer almost always lacks. Hence the written word in its limited effect will in general serve more to retain, to reinforce, to deepen, a point of view or opinion that is already present. Really great historical changes are not induced by the *written* word, but at most *accompanied* by it. . . .

The mass meeting is also necessary for the reason that in it the individual, who at first, while becoming a supporter of a young movement, feels lonely and easily succumbs to the fear of being alone, for the first time gets the picture of a larger community, which in most people has a strengthening, encouraging effect. The same man, within a company or a battalion, surrounded by all his comrades, would set out on an attack with a lighter heart than if left entirely on his own. In the crowd he always feels somewhat sheltered, even if a thousand reasons argue against it.

But the community of the great demonstration not only strengthens the individual, it also unites and helps to create an *esprit de corps*. The man who is exposed to grave tribulations, as the first advocate of a new doctrine in his factory or workshop, absolutely needs that strengthening which lies in the conviction of being a member and fighter in a great comprehensive body. And he obtains an impression of this body for the first time in the mass demonstration. When from his little workshop or big factory, in which he feels very small, he steps for the first time into a mass meeting and has thousands and thousands of people of the same opinions around him, when, as a seeker, he is swept away by three or four thousand others into the mighty effect of suggestive intoxication and enthusiasm, when the visible success and agreement of thousands confirm to him the rightness of the new doctrine and for the first time arouse doubt in the truth of his previous conviction – then he himself has succumbed to the magic influence of what we designate as 'mass suggestion'. The will, the longing, and also the power of thousands are accumulated in every individual. . . .

Adolf Hitler, *Mein Kampf*, with an introduction by D. C. Watt, 1969, pp 430–2, 435

Questions

a   What point is Hitler making about the timing of public meetings?
b   What is the rôle of the speaker at these meetings?
c   Why did Hitler claim that oratory was more powerful than the written word?
d   What indications are apparent of the part played by psychology in the appeal of Nazism?
*   e   Examine the contribution of Nazi meetings to the rise of the party in the 1920s.

3   Conversion

Hitler was delivering an address to the students of Berlin University and the Institute of Technology. My students urged me to attend. Not yet convinced, but already uncertain of my ground, I went along. The site of the meeting was a beer hall called the Hasenheide. Dirty walls, narrow
5   stairs and an ill-kept interior created a poverty-stricken atmosphere. This was a place where workmen ordinarily held beer parties. The room was overcrowded. It seemed as if nearly all the students in Berlin wanted to see and hear this man whom his adherents so much admired and his opponents so much detested. A large number of professors sat in favoured
10   places in the middle of a bare platform. Their presence gave the meeting an importance and a social acceptability that it would not otherwise have had. Our group had also secured good seats on the platform, not far from the lectern.

Hitler entered and was tempestuously hailed by his numerous
15   followers among the students. This enthusiasm in itself made a great impression upon me. But his appearance also surprised me. On posters and in caricatures I had seen him in military tunic, with shoulder straps, swastika armband, and hair flapping over his forehead. But here he was wearing a well-fitted blue suit and looking markedly respectable.
20   Everything about him bore out the note of reasonable modesty. Later I learned that he had a great gift for adjusting — consciously or intuitively — to his surroundings.

As the ovation went on for minutes he tried, as if slightly pained, to check it. Then, in a low voice, hesitantly and somewhat shyly, he began a
25   kind of historical lecture rather than a speech. To me there was something engaging about it — all the more so since it ran counter to everything the propaganda of his opponents had led me to expect: a hysterical demagogue, a shrieking and gesticulating fanatic in uniform. He did not allow the bursts of applause to tempt him away from his sober
30   tone.

It seemed as if he were candidly presenting his anxieties about the future. His irony was softened by a somewhat self-conscious humor; his South German charm reminded me agreeably of my native region. A cool Prussian could never have captivated me that way. Hitler's initial
35   shyness soon disappeared, at times now his pitch rose. He spoke urgently and with hypnotic persuasiveness. The mood he cast was much deeper than the speech itself, most of which I did not remember for long.

Moreover, I was carried on the wave of the enthusiasm which, one could almost feel this physically, bore the speaker along from sentence to
40   sentence. It swept away any skepticism, any reservations. Opponents were given no chance to speak. This furthered the illusion, at least momentarily, of unanimity. Finally, Hitler no longer seemed to be speaking to convince; rather, he seemed to feel that he was expressing what the audience, by now transformed into a single mass, expected of

45   him. It was as if it were the most natural thing in the world to lead students and part of the faculty of the two greatest academies in Germany submissively by a leash. Yet that evening he was not yet the absolute ruler, immune from all criticism, but was still exposed to attacks from all directions. . . .

50   Here, it seemed to me, was hope. Here were new ideals, a new understanding, new tasks. . . . The peril of communism, which seemed inexorably on its way, could be checked, Hitler persuaded us, and instead of hopeless unemployment, Germany could move toward economic recovery. He had mentioned the Jewish problem peripherally. But such

55   remarks did not worry me, although I was not an anti-Semite; . . .

Both Goebbels and Hitler had understood how to unleash mass instincts at their meetings, how to play on the passions that underlay the veneer of ordinary respectable life. Practised demagogues, they succeeded in fusing the assembled workers, petits bourgeois, and students into a

60   homogeneous mob whose opinions they could mold as they pleased. . . . But as I see it today, these politicians in particular were in fact molded by the mob itself, guided by its yearnings and its day-dreams. Of course Goebbels and Hitler knew how to penetrate through to the instincts of their audiences; but in the deeper sense they derived their whole existence

65   from these audiences. Certainly the masses roared to the beat set by Hitler's and Goebbels's baton; yet they were not the true conductors. The mob determined the theme. To compensate for misery, insecurity, unemployment, and hopelessness, this anonymous assemblage wallowed for hours at a time in obsessions, savagery, license. This was no ardent

70   nationalism. Rather, for a few short hours the personal unhappiness caused by the breakdown of the economy was replaced by a frenzy that demanded victims. And Hitler and Goebbels threw them the victims. By lashing out at their opponents and vilifying the Jews they gave expression and direction to fierce, primal passions. . . .

75   The following day I applied for membership in the National Socialist Party and in January 1931 became Member Number 474.481. . . .

I did see quite a number of rough spots in the party doctrines. But I assumed that they would be polished in time, as has often happened in the history of other revolutions. The crucial fact appeared to me to be that I

80   personally had to choose between a future Communist Germany or a future National Socialist Germany since the political center between these antipodes had melted away. Moreover, in 1931, I had some reason to feel that Hitler was moving in a moderate direction. I did not realize that there were opportunistic reasons for this. Hitler was trying to appear

85   respectable in order to seem qualified to enter the government. . . .

In making this decision to join the accursed party, I had for the first time denied my own past, my upper-middle-class origins, and my previous environment. Far more than I suspected, the 'time of decision' was already past for me. I felt, in Martin Buber's phrase, 'anchored in

90   responsibility in a party.' My inclination to be relieved of having to think, particularly about unpleasant facts, helped to sway the balance. In this I

did not differ from millions of others. Such mental slackness above all facilitated, established, and finally assured the success of the National Socialist system. . . .

A. Speer, *Inside the Third Reich*, 1971, pp 15–17, 19–20

Questions

a   How was the meeting at 'the Hasenheide' (line 4) given social acceptability?

b   In what ways was Speer affected by seeing Hitler in person for the first time? How does he explain his reactions?

c   What did Buber mean by the phrase 'anchored in responsibility in a party' (lines 89–90)?

d   Do you think that Speer is trying to exculpate himself in his account of his 'conversion' to Nazism?

*   e   What was Speer's role in National Socialist Germany in the period 1933–45?

4   The Party Rallies

Nobody who has not witnessed the various displays given at Nuremberg during the week's rally, or been subjected to the atmosphere thereat, can be said to be fully acquainted with the Nazi movement in Germany. . . .

The displays themselves were most impressive. That of the Party
5   leaders (or heads of the Party organisation in towns and villages throughout the country) took place in the evening at eight p.m., in the stadium or Zeppelinfield. Dressed in their brown shirts, these 140,000 men were drawn up in six great columns, with passages between them, mostly in the stadium itself, but filling also the tiers of seats surrounding
10   the stadium and facing the elevated platform reserved for the Chancellor, his Ministers and his guards, the massed bands, official guests, and other spectators. Hitler himself arrived at the far entrance of the stadium, some 400 yards from the platform, and, accompanied by several hundred of his followers, marched on foot up the central passage to his appointed place.
15   His arrival was theatrically notified by the sudden turning into the air of the 300 or more searchlights with which the stadium was surrounded. The blue-tinged light from these met thousands of feet up in the sky at the top to make a kind of square roof, to which a chance cloud gave added realism. The effect, which was both solemn and beautiful, was like being
20   inside a cathedral of ice. At the word of command the standard-bearers then advanced from out of sight at the far end, up the main lane, and over the further tiers and up the four side lanes. A certain proportion of these standards had electric lights on their shafts, and the spectacle of these five rivers of red and gold rippling forward under the dome of blue light, in
25   complete silence, through the massed formations of brownshirts, was indescribably picturesque. I had spent six years in St. Petersburg before

the war in the best days of the old Russian ballet, but for grandiose beauty
I have never seen a ballet to compare with it. The German, who has a
highly developed herd instinct, is perfectly happy when he is wearing a
30 uniform, marching in step, and singing a chorus, and the Nazi revolution
has certainly known how to appeal to these instincts in his nature. As a
display of aggregate strength it was ominous; as a triumph of mass
organisation combined with beauty it was superb.

    Sir Nevile Henderson, *Failure of a Mission, Berlin 1937–1939*,
    1940, pp 70–71

Questions

a   What were the 'brownshirts' (line 25)?
b   What elements of military display were evident at the rallies?
c   How were drama and theatre injected into the Zeppelinfield?
* d   Goebbels said that Hitler changed the German man from 'a little
      worm into part of a large dragon'. What was the significance of party
      marches and rallies in this?
* e   In what ways did the Nazis use visual media for propaganda?

5   One Community's Experience

By the end of the winter of 1931–32, conditions in Thalburg were
favourable to the rapid advance of Nazism. The depression was at its
worst, violence was becoming more frequent, and the twin passions of
nationalism and class antagonism were at their height. Thalburg's Nazis
5 had established themselves as both respectable and radical. They were
seen as patriotic, anti-socialist and religious. They enjoyed the apparent
blessings of the conservatives. But at the same time the Nazis appeared to
be vigorous, determined, and, above all, ready to use radical means to
deal with the crucial problem – the depression . . . only extreme
10 measures would end the depression and only the Nazis were thought of as
sufficiently extreme. . . .

    . . . there was no Nazi *coup d'état*. Instead, there was a series of quasi-
legal actions over a period of at least six months, no one of which by itself
constituted a revolution, but the sum of which transformed Germany
15 from a republic to a dictatorship. The problem was where to draw the
line. But by the time the line could be clearly drawn, the revolution was a
fait accompli, the potential organs of resistance had been individually
smashed, and organized resistance was no longer possible. . . .

    What, then, is to be learned from Thalburg's experience in the years
20 1930 to 1935, the years of the Nazi seizure of power?

    In the first place, it is clear that an essential arena in the Nazi electoral
surge and the seizure of power was on the local level. Thalburg's Nazis
created their own image by their own initiative, vigor, and propaganda.
They knew exactly what needed to be done to effect the transfer of power
25 to themselves in the spring of 1933, and they did it apparently without

more than generalized directives from above. Exactly how much was initiated locally and how much was promoted by the example of other Nazi groups in other towns or by the District and national Nazi leadership remains to be determined. . . . But it was in the hundreds of localities like Thalburg all over Germany that the revolution was made actual. They formed the foundation of the Third Reich.

As for the reasons behind the particular experience in Thalburg, the most important factor in the victory of Nazism was the active division of the town along class lines. Though there was cohesion in Thalburg before the Nazis began their campaigns leading to the seizure of power, the cohesion existed within the middle class or within the working class and did not extend to the town as a whole. The victory of Nazism can be explained to a large extent by the desire on the part of Thalburg's middle class to suppress the lower class and especially its political representatives, the Social Democratic party.

This is why Thalburgers rejoiced in the gains of the Nazis, and this is why they applauded the institution of the dictatorship. The antipathy of the middle class was not directed towards individual members of the SPD, but only toward the organization itself; not toward the working class as such, but only toward its political and social aspirations; not, finally, toward the reality of the SPD, but mainly toward a myth which they nurtured about the SPD. For a variety of reasons, Thalburg's middle class was so intent on dealing a blow to the Social Democrats that it could not see that the instrument it chose would one day be turned against itself. . . .

Yet it would be incorrect to place all the blame upon Thalburg's Social Democracy. The middle class responded to the existence of the SPD in ways which were almost paranoid. Its members insisted upon viewing the SPD as a 'Marxist' party at a time when this was no longer so. They were determined to turn the clock back to a period when the organized working class was forcibly kept from exerting influence. They felt threatened by the very existence of this organization. This view of the SPD was not in accord with reality, since by any objective standard the goal of the SPD in Thalburg was to maintain the kind of town that Thalburg's middle class itself wanted.

Perhaps the behavior of the good burghers of Thalburg becomes more understandable when one realizes the extent to which they were committed to nationalism. The excess of patriotic feeling in the town during the pre-Hitler period was the great moral wedge for Nazism. In many ways the actions and beliefs of Thalburgers during the last years of the Weimar era were the same as if World War I had never ended. It was in this sort of atmosphere that the SPD might seem treasonable and the Nazi reasonable.

A similar effect was wrought by the depression. While Thalburg's middle class was not decisively affected by the economic crisis, the burghers were made desperate through fear and through an obsession with the effects of the depression, especially the sight of the unemployed.

As for the effect of the depression upon the lower classes, it was equally large. There is no doubt that the progressive despair of the jobless, as reflected in the longer and longer periods of unemployment, weakened the forces of democracy in the town. . . .

But the main effect of the depression was to radicalize the town. In the face of the mounting economic crisis, Thalburgers were willing to tolerate approaches that would have left them indignant or indifferent under other circumstances. Thus the disgusting and debilitating party acrimony and violence mushroomed in the years before the dictatorship. The extent of the violence in Thalburg was an expression of the radical situation, but it also added to it by making violence normal and acceptable. With the growing nationalism and increasing impatience over the depression, violence and political tension were significant factors in preparing the town for the Nazi takeover.

All these factors were exploited with considerable astuteness by Nazi propaganda. In the face of the senseless round of political squabbling and fecklessness, the Nazis presented the appearance of a unified, purposeful, and vigorous alternative. Their propaganda played upon all the needs and fears of the town and directed itself to almost every potential group of adherents. By their own efforts the Nazis captured the allegiance of the confused and troubled middle class.

This set the stage for the actual seizure of power, but the revolution itself was also conducted in such a way as to insure success. The fact that this was, in the words of Konrad Heiden, a '*coup d'état* by instalments' kept the *Reichsbanner* from responding at any one point. By the time the SPD had been broken, the terror system had been inaugurated, largely through social reinforcement.

The single biggest factor in this process was the destruction of society in Thalburg. What social cohesion there was in the town existed in the club life, and this was destroyed in the early months of Nazi rule. With their social organizations gone and with terror a reality, Thalburgers were isolated from one another. This was true of the middle class but even more true of the workers, since by the destruction of the SPD and the unions the whole complex of social ties created by this super-club was effaced. By reducing the people of Thalburg to unconnected social atoms, the Nazis could move the resulting mass in whatever direction they wished. The process was probably easier in Thalburg than in most other places, since the town contained so many government employees. . . . Especially Thalburg's teachers — who formed the social and cultural elite of the town — found themselves drawn into support of the NSDAP almost immediately.

Beyond this, the Nazis took considerable action to strengthen support, especially in the early months. There were the constant parades and meetings which gave the impression of irresistible enthusiasm and approval. There was the vigor in the economic area which more than anything else seemed to justify the dictatorship. But in addition to Nazi efforts on their own behalf, there were other factors which favored them.

120 Many signs indicate that the depression was slowly curing itself by 1933. Moreover, there was the public works money allocated under the previous regime but available just as the Nazis came to power. And one should probably also take into account the fact that the essential work of establishing the dictatorship came during the spring – a time when
125 enthusiasm seems appropriate and revolution not wholly unnatural.

Thus many factors combined to make Nazism a possibility for Thalburg. At the same time the town itself influenced the nature of Nazism as it manifested itself locally. It seems probable, for example, that the general lack of violence during the first months of the Third Reich
130 was due to the nature of Thalburg as a small town. Much as the Nazis hated all that the Socialists stood for, both sides knew each other too well for cold and systematic violence to occur. The SA might be willing to pummel their neighbors in a street fight, but they seemed to shrink from attacking the Socialists when they were defenseless. This is not to say that
135 no violence took place, but it does help explain the fact that no one was killed and no one sent to a concentration camp from Thalburg during the early years of the Nazi regime. . . .

Ultimately almost every Thalburger came to understand the Third Reich. Most Thalburgers learned what a dictatorship meant when they
140 sensed the general breakdown of trust and social communication. All became aware of it when Hitler's policies brought war to them. Despite the super-patriotism in the pre-Nazi years, there was no cheering in the streets when the Thalburg battalion marched out of town in 1939. The war brought hunger with it, especially after 1945, and the sons of many
145 Thalburgers learned to temper their love of militarism on the cold steppes of Russia.

But no one foresaw these consequences in the days when Thalburg's middle class was voting overwhelmingly for the introduction of the Third Reich. And that, perhaps, is the most significant lesson of all to be
150 gained from Thalburg's experiences during and prior to the Nazi seizure of power. Hardly anyone in Thalburg in those days grasped what was happening. There was no real comprehension of what the town would experience if Hitler came to power, no real understanding of what Nazism was. . . .
155 The problem of Nazism was primarily a problem of perception. . . .

W. S. Allen, *The Nazi Seizure of Power*, 1965, pp 84–5, 180, 274–8, 280–1 [Based on Northeim, Lower Saxony, and given the fictional name of Thalburg]

Questions

a Explain 'NSDAP' (line 112); 'SPD' (line 44); *'coup d'état'* (line 12).
b Why were the Nazis successful in this community?
c What were the defects of the SPD in Thalburg?
d In what ways did the depression contribute to Nazi success?
* e Explain Heiden's phrase, a *'coup d'état'* by instalments' (line 96).

*   *f*   What relevance has the Nazi experience in Thalburg to democracies today?

Further Work

a   'Where Hitler's evil genius lay was in revealing only that part of his purpose that would appeal broadly to the German people while concealing from them what they might disapprove of. His success depended on the extent to which he could persuade the German people that he was no more than the instrument of *their desires*. That he could articulate and deliver what *they wanted*. The truth was the reverse.' (J. A. S. Grenville)
Assess the validity of this viewpoint with reference to Hitler's aims and policies before and after 1933.

b   Anti-semitism was one of the main features of National Socialism. What were its origins, and why did it find support among many of the German people in the inter-war period?

c   'To the true fascist, man was irrational and violent, reason an excuse for hesitation and a sign of emotional shallowness. Action mattered above all else and action sprang from the heart and from the blood.' (A. Milward)
'The Nazis represented a new barbarism, not another political movement.' (J. A. S. Grenville)
Was National Socialism a reversion to primitive instincts, and therefore inaccessible to rational investigation by historians?

d   Which other European countries had successful Fascist movements between the wars? What were the common features of these right-wing movements?

e   What was the response in Britain to the rise of the NSDAP? How and why did this change from 1933?

f   In one of his speeches Hitler said, 'the weak must be chiselled away . . . I want a violent, arrogant, unafraid, cruel youth who must be able to suffer pain. Nothing weak or tender must be left in them. Their eyes must bespeak once again the free, magnificent beast of prey.' Examine the rôle of youth in the Nazi movement.

VIII   The Origins of the
          Second World War

Introduction

The last twenty years have experienced two seismic shocks on the origins of the two World Wars of this century, both caused by attempts to demolish accepted notions: the German historian Fritz Fischer got into serious trouble for suggesting that the leaders of Germany caused the First World War, while A. J. P. Taylor was censured for apparently saying that Hitler did *not* cause the second. Taylor's thesis provoked a bitter and acrimonious debate which to many of his critics seemed to confirm what they thought: his book was an 'academic exercise' to show that using the same evidence one could reach a radically different conclusion from previously accepted versions. Close scrutiny of Taylor's book is essential, and the reader will reap a rich reward from the early, largely uncontroversial, chapters.

The debate is a useful one for clarifying the interaction between events and the plans of human beings. Taylor stresses the importance in the origins of World War II of profound causes and specific events, but his book is more about the latter, for which he has been criticised by T. W. Mason and F. H. Hinsley. This is a fundamental flaw in Taylor's book, for, as Alan Milward wrote, 'The military strategy of Germany, her economic organization and her pre-war diplomacy are all of a piece, they went together. And they were all influenced very heavily by, indeed were in some cases actually the product of, the ideology of the National Socialist Party.' This is why the famous Hossbach Memorandum can apparently be interpreted in several ways; without the context of National Socialism, however, it loses much of its impact.

The rôle of Britain and France is also an issue, as is the post-Versailles international situation. To what extent did appeasement 'cause' the Second World War? There are many fascinating interwoven problems for the historian in this debate, which will demand the skills of analysis and synthesis. Is it still tenable to say, with H. R. Trevor-Roper, that 'The Second World War was Hitler's personal war in many senses. He intended it, he prepared for it, he chose the moment for launching it. . . .'?

Further Reading

A. Adamthwaite (ed.), *The Making of the Second World War*, Allen &

Unwin, 1977, a very informative set of documents with a lucid 100-page introduction, particularly suitable for a depth study at 'A' Level.

W. Carr, *Arms, Autarky and Aggression*, Edward Arnold, 1972, a modern appraisal of the 1930s, with a good discussion of rearmament.

W. R. Louis (ed.), *The Origins of the Second World War: A. J. P. Taylor and His Critics*, Wiley, 1972, a historiographical and fairly light review of the debate.

A. Marwick and A. Adamthwaite, *Between Two Wars*, 1973 (Open University Arts Course 'War and Society', Units 19–20).

A. Milward, A. Marwick and M. R. D. Foot, *World War II*, 1973 (Open University Arts Course 'War and Society', Units 21–3).

E. M. Robertson (ed.), *The Origins of the Second World War*, Macmillan, 1971, more stimulating than Louis' review, with valuable contributions from Trevor-Roper, Mason and Bullock.

A. J. P. Taylor, *The Origins of the Second World War*, Penguin edn., 1963, a stimulating but highly controversial work.

A. J. P. Taylor and T. W. Mason, *The Origins of World War II*, 1973 (Open University Arts Course 'War and Society' radio programme 10).

C. Thorne, *The Approach of War, 1938–9*, Macmillan, 1967, a straightforward general account.

1 Hitler's Aims?

Indeed, we can justly say that the whole life struggle of a people in truth consists in safeguarding the territory it requires as a general prerequisite for the sustenance of the increasing population. . . .

5   In the life of nations there are several ways for correcting the disproportion between population and territory. The most natural way is to adapt the soil, from time to time, to the increased population. This requires a determination to fight and the risk of bloodshed. But this very bloodshed is also the only one that can be justified to the people. Since through it the necessary space is won for the further increase of a people, it
10   automatically finds manifold compensation for the humanity staked on the battlefield. Thus the bread of freedom grows from the hardships of war. The sword was the path-breaker for the plough. . . .

     Furthermore, there is no spot on this earth that has been determined as the abode of a people for all time, since the rule of nature has for tens of
15   thousands of years forced mankind eternally to migrate. . . .

     A healthy foreign policy, therefore, will always keep the winning of the basis of a people's sustenance immovably in sight as its ultimate goal. Domestic policy must secure the inner strength of a people so that it can assert itself in the sphere of foreign policy. Foreign policy must secure the
20   life of a people for its domestic political development. Hence domestic policy and foreign policy are not only most closely linked, but must also mutually complement one another. . . .

The National Socialist movement, on the contrary, will always let its
foreign policy be determined by the necessity to secure the space
necessary to the life of our people. . . .

Above all, however, only through a territorial policy in Europe can the
human resources shifted there be preserved for our people, including
their military utilization. An additional 500,000 square kilometers in
Europe can provide new homesteads for millions of German peasants,
and make available millions of soldiers to the power of the German
people for the moment of decision.

The only area in Europe that could be considered for such a territorial
policy therefore was Russia. The thinly settled western border regions
which already once had received German colonists as bringers of culture,
could likewise be considered for the new territorial policy of the German
nation. . . .

The great domestic task of the future lies in the elimination of these
general symptoms of the decay of our people. This is the mission of the
National Socialist movement. A new nation must arise from this work
which overcomes even the worst evils of the present, the cleavage
between the classes, for which the bourgeoisie and Marxism are equally
guilty.

The aim of this reform work of a domestic political kind must finally
be the regaining of our people's strength for the prosecution of its
struggle for existence and thereby the strength to represent its vital
interests abroad. . . .

But now there remains the question of just what meaning a German —
Russian alliance should have in general. Only the one of preserving
Russia from destruction and sacrificing Germany for that? Regardless of
how this alliance would turn out in the end, Germany could not arrive at
setting a decisive foreign policy goal. For thereby nothing would be
changed regarding the fundamental vital question, indeed regarding the
vital needs, of our people. On the contrary Germany, thereby, would be
more than ever cut off from the only rational territorial policy in order to
pad out her future with the scuffle over unimportant border adjustments.
For the question of space for our people cannot be solved either in the
west or in the south of Europe. . . .

For the future an alliance of Germany with Russia has no sense for
Germany, neither from the standpoint of sober expediency nor from that
of human community. On the contrary, it is good fortune for the future
that this development has taken place in just this way because thereby a
spell has been broken which would have prevented us from seeking the
goal of German foreign policy there where it solely and exclusively can
lie: territory in the East. . . .

Germany decides to go over to [her future aim] a clear farseeing
territorial policy. Thereby she abandons all attempts at world-industry
and world-trade and instead concentrates all her strength in order,
through the allotment of sufficient living space for the next hundred years
to our people, also to prescribe a path of life. Since this territory can be

70 only in the East, the obligation to be a naval power also recedes into the background. Germany tries anew to champion her interests through the formation of a decisive power on land.

This aim is equally in keeping with the highest national as well as folkish requirements. It likewise presupposes great military power means
75 for its execution, but does not necessarily bring Germany into conflict with all European great powers. As surely as France here will remain Germany's enemy, just as little does the nature of such a political aim contain a reason for England, and especially for Italy, to maintain the enmity of the World War. . . .
80 We will also never sacrifice the blood of our people in order to bring about small border rectifications, but only for territory in order to win a further expansion and sustenance for our people. This aim drives us eastward. . . .

Once our people, however, will have grasped this great geopolitical
85 aim in the East the consequences will not only be clarity regarding German foreign policy but also stability. . . .

Germany then, also domestically, will have to take steps toward the strongest concentration of her means of power. She will have to realize that armies and navies are set up and organized not along romantic lines
90 but according to practical requirements. Then she will automatically select as our greatest task the formation of a superior strong land army since our future as a matter of fact does not lie on the water, but in Europe rather. . . .

It is the foreign policy task of the National Socialist movement to
95 prepare and ultimately to carry out this development. It must also place foreign policy in the service of the reorganization of our folkdom on the basis of its philosophical range of ideas. . . .

> *Hitler's Secret Book*, with introduction by T. Taylor, New York,
> 1962, pp 14—15, 34, 45, 74, 79, 134—5, 139, 145, 195, 210

Questions

a What does Hitler see as the mainstay of 'a healthy foreign policy' (line 16)?

b What evidence is there of the desire for 'lebensraum'? Where would this 'living space' be found?

c When he wrote this, did Hitler envisage conflict with the victors of the First World War in implementing his aims?

d The book was written about 1928, but remained unpublished until 1961. Why was this? How valid is it as primary evidence on the aims of German foreign policy from 1933 to 1939?

* e What links are discernible between Hitler's assertions and those of Mason's article in extract 4?

* f To what extent was Social Darwinism a major part of Hitler's intellectual make-up?

2 The Hossbach Memorandum

MINUTES OF THE CONFERENCE IN THE REICH CHANCELLERY, BERLIN, NOVEMBER 5, 1937, FROM 4.15 TO 8.30 P.M. . . .

The Führer began by stating that the subject of the present conference was
5   of such importance that its discussion would, in other countries, certainly be a matter for a full Cabinet meeting, but he — the Führer — had rejected the idea of making it a subject of discussion before the wider circle of the Reich Cabinet just because of the importance of the matter. His exposition to follow was the fruit of thorough deliberation and the
10   experience of his 4½ years of power. He wished to explain to the gentlemen present his basic ideas concerning the opportunities for the development of our position in the field of foreign affairs and its requirements, and he asked, in the interests of a long-term German policy, that his exposition be regarded, in the event of his death, as his last
15   will and testament.

The Führer then continued:

The aim of German policy was to make secure and to preserve the racial community [*Volksmasse*] and to enlarge it. It was therefore a question of space. . . .
20   German policy had to reckon with two hate-inspired antagonists, Britain and France, to whom a German colossus in the center of Europe was a thorn in the flesh, and both countries were opposed to any further strengthening of Germany's position either in Europe or overseas; . . .

Germany's problem could only be solved by means of force and this
25   was never without attendant risk. . . . If one accepts as the basis of the following exposition the resort to force with its attendant risks, then there remain still to be answered the questions 'when' and 'how'. In this matter there were three cases [*Falle*] to be dealt with:

Case 1: Period 1943—1945
30   After this date only a change for the worse, from our point of view, could be expected.

The equipment of the army, navy, and *Luftwaffe*, as well as the formation of the officer corps, was nearly completed. Equipment and armament were modern; in further delay there lay the danger of their
35   obsolescence. In particular, the secrecy of 'special weapons' could not be preserved forever. The recruiting of reserves was limited to current age groups; further drafts from older untrained age groups were no longer available.

Our relative strength would decrease in relation to the rearmament
40   which would by then have been carried out by the rest of the world. If we did not act by 1943—45, any year could, in consequence of a lack of reserves, produce the food crisis, to cope with which the necessary foreign exchange was not available, and this must be regarded as a 'waning point of the regime.' Besides, the world was expecting our attack and was
45   increasing its counter-measures from year to year. It was while the rest of

the world was still preparing its defences [*sich abriegele*] that we were obliged to take the offensive.

Nobody knew today what the situation would be in the years 1943–45. One thing only was certain, that we could not wait longer.

On the one hand there was the great *Wehrmacht*, and the necessity of maintaining it at its present level, the aging of the movement and of its leaders; and on the other, the prospect of a lowering of the standard of living and of a limitation of the birth rate, which left no choice but to act. If the Führer was still living, it was his unalterable resolve to solve Germany's problem of space at the latest by 1943–45. The necessity for action before 1943–45 would arise in cases 2 and 3.

Case 2:

If internal strife in France should develop into such a domestic crisis as to absorb the French Army completely and render it incapable of use for war against Germany, then the time for action against the Czechs had come.

Case 3:

If France is so embroiled by a war with another state that she cannot 'proceed' against Germany.

For the improvement of our politico-military position our first objective, in the event of our being embroiled in war, must be to overthrow Czechoslovakia and Austria simultaneously in order to remove the threat to our flank in any possible operation against the West. In a conflict with France it was hardly to be regarded as likely that the Czechs would declare war on us on the very same day as France. The desire to join in the war would, however, increase among the Czechs in proportion to any weakening on our part and then her participation could clearly take the form of an attack toward Silesia, toward the north or toward the west. . . .

Actually, the Führer believed that almost certainly Britain, and probably France as well, had already tacitly written off the Czechs and were reconciled to the fact that this question would be cleared up in due course by Germany. Difficulties connected with the Empire, and the prospect of being once more entangled in a protracted European war, were decisive considerations for Britain against participation in a war against Germany. Britain's attitude would certainly not be without influence on that of France. An attack by France without British support, and with the prospect of the offensive being brought to a standstill on our western fortifications, was hardly probable. . . . And . . . it had to be remembered that the defence measures of the Czechs were growing in strength from year to year, and that the actual worth of the Austrian Army also was increasing in the course of time. Even though the populations concerned, especially of Czechoslovakia, were not sparse, the annexation of Czechoslovakia and Austria would mean an acquisition of foodstuffs for 5 to 6 million people, on the assumption that the compulsory emigration of 2 million people from Czechoslovakia and 1 million people from Austria was practicable. . . .

Italy was not expected to object to the elimination of the Czechs, but it was impossible at the moment to estimate what her attitude on the Austrian question would be; that depended essentially upon whether the Duce were still alive.

The degree of surprise and the swiftness of our action were decisive factors for Poland's attitude. Poland – with Russia at her rear – will have little inclination to engage in war against a victorious Germany.

Military intervention by Russia must be countered by the swiftness of our operations; however, whether such an intervention was a practical contingency at all was, in view of Japan's attitude, more than doubtful.

Should case 2 arise – the crippling of France by civil war – the situation thus created by the elimination of the most dangerous opponent must be seized upon *whenever it occurs* for the blow against the Czechs.

The Führer saw case 3 coming definitely nearer; it might emerge from the present tensions in the Mediterranean, and he was resolved to take advantage of it whenever it happened, even as early as 1938. . . .

If Germany made use of this war to settle the Czech and Austrian questions, it was to be assumed that Britain – herself at war with Italy – would decide not to act against Germany. Without British support, a warlike action by France against Germany was not to be expected. . . .

The second part of the conference was concerned with concrete questions of armament.

HOSSBACH

'The Hossbach Memorandum', *Documents on German Foreign Policy, 1918–1945*, H.M.S.O., 1949, Series D, vol I, pp 29–30

Questions

a Explain 'Germany's problem of space' (line 55); 'internal strife in France' (line 58).

b What evidence is there in the document to indicate how important the meeting was rated by Hitler?

c In what circumstances did Hitler envisage conflict in Europe? Did any of these actually take place and, if not, does that invalidate the document?

d How did Hitler view the relationship between Britain and France? Was he correct?

* e What light does the Memorandum throw on events in Europe in 1938–9?

* f 'Beware of documents' (Clemenceau). What context is needed to see the Hossbach Memorandum in perspective?

3 'Taylor's Law'

The watershed between the two world wars extended over precisely two years. Post-war ended when Germany reoccupied the Rhineland on 7

March 1936; pre-war began when she annexed Austria on 13 March 1938. From that moment, change and upheaval went on almost without interruption until the representatives of the Powers, victorious in the second World war, met at Potsdam in July 1945. Who first raised the storm and launched the march of events? The accepted answer is clear: it was Hitler. The moment of his doing so is also accepted: it was on 5 November 1937. We have a record of the statements which he made that day. It is called 'the Hossbach memorandum', after the man who made it. This record is supposed to reveal Hitler's plans. Much play was made with it at Nuremberg; and the editors of the *Documents on German Foreign Policy* say that 'it provides a summary of German foreign policy in 1937–38'. It is therefore worth looking at in detail. Perhaps we shall find in it the explanation of the second World war; or perhaps we shall find only the source of a legend. . . .

Hitler's exposition was in large part day-dreaming, unrelated to what followed in real life. Even if seriously meant, it was not a call to action, at any rate not to the action of a great war; it was a demonstration that a great war would not be necessary. Despite the preliminary talk about 1943–1945, its solid core was the examination of the chances for peaceful triumphs in 1938, when France would be preoccupied elsewhere. Hitler's listeners remained doubtful. The generals insisted that the French army would be superior to the German even if engaged against Italy as well. Neurath doubted whether a Mediterranean conflict between France and Italy were imminent. Hitler waved these doubts aside: 'He was convinced of Britain's non-participation, and therefore he did not believe in the probability of belligerent action by France against Germany.' There is only one safe conclusion to be drawn from this rambling disquisition: Hitler was gambling on some twist of fortune which would present him with success in foreign affairs, just as a miracle had made him Chancellor in 1933. There was here no concrete plan, no directive for German policy in 1937 and 1938. Or if there were a directive, it was to wait upon events.

Why then did Hitler hold this conference? This question was not asked at Nuremberg; it has not been asked by historians. Yet surely it is an elementary part of historical discipline to ask of a document not only what is in it, but why it came into existence. The conference of 5 November 1937 was a curious gathering. Only Goering was a Nazi. The others were old-style Conservatives who had remained in office to keep Hitler under control; all of them except Raeder were to be dismissed from their posts within three months. Hitler knew that all except Goering were his opponents; and he did not trust Goering much. Why did he reveal his inmost thoughts to men whom he distrusted and whom he was shortly to discharge? This question has an easy answer: he did not reveal his inmost thoughts. There was no crisis in foreign policy to provoke a broad discussion or sweeping decisions. . . .

. . . none of the men who attended the meeting on 5 November gave it another thought until Goering found the record produced against him at Nuremberg as evidence of his war guilt. From that moment it has

haunted the corridors of historical research. It is the basis for the view that
there is nothing to be discovered about the origins of the second World
war. Hitler, it is claimed, decided on war, and planned it in detail on 5
November 1937. Yet the Hossbach memorandum contains no plans of
the kind, and would never have been supposed to do so, unless it had been
displayed at Nuremberg. The memorandum tells us, what we know
already, that Hitler (like every other German statesman) intended
Germany to become the dominant Power in Europe. It also tells us that he
speculated how this might happen. His speculations were mistaken. They
bear hardly any relation to the actual outbreak of war in 1939. A racing
tipster who only reached Hitler's level of accuracy would not do well for
his clients . . . .

> A. J. P. Taylor, *The Origins of the Second World War*, 1963 edn, pp
> 168–72

Questions

a   Identify 'Nuremberg' (line 12); 'Neurath' (line 25); 'Raeder' (line
40); 'Goering' (line 38).

b   Does Taylor think Hitler had no plans for the future?

c   Is it true to say 'that Hitler (like every other German statesman)
intended Germany to become the dominant Power in Europe' (lines
56–7)?

d   Taylor has often been criticised for oversimplifying complex
problems. Are there any examples here?

e   ' "Taylor's Law" – documents do not really signify anything.' (F. H.
Hinsley) Is the viewpoint of Taylor on the Hossbach Memorandum
an example of this?

4   A Critique of Taylor

One of the major themes of Mr Taylor's book is the inability of historians
writing on the inter-war period to overcome their horror at the atrocities
committed by the National Socialist regime; this horror has led them to
mistake the general moral responsibility of the Third Reich for the
greatest barbarities in the history of western civilisation for an assumed,
concrete historical responsibility for the outbreak of the Second World
War. There is certainly much truth in this contention, and Mr Taylor has
made a greater effort than any previous historian to achieve an emotional
and moral detachment from the subject-matter. . . .

It is no coincidence, however, that the best passages in Mr Taylor's
book are those which deal with countries other than Germany, countries
whose foreign policies were basically pragmatic, and whose statesmen
were seeking more or less limited goals with more or less conventional
means. It is the basic unspoken postulate of *The Origins of the Second World
War* that the foreign policy of the Third Reich was also of this character.

In attempting to lift the shadow cast by the Nuremberg tribunals over the historiography of Nazi Germany, Mr Taylor reduces the international relations of the period to the obsolete formula of independent states pursuing intelligible national interests with varying degrees of diplomatic
20 skill. 'What happened' is by this token the story of the complex interaction of these national policies, an interaction so complex and so swiftly changing that no statesman could come near to grasping it in its entirety; and the answer to the question 'why' lies largely in these inevitable shortcomings of the statesmen.
25 'The Second World War, too, had profound causes; but it also grew out of specific events, and these events are worth detailed examination.' Yet Mr Taylor's formula largely excludes the profound causes from consideration; it seems unable to accommodate political movements and ideologies. National Socialism was perhaps the profoundest cause of the
30 Second World War, but Mr Taylor's book is not informed by any conception of the distinctive character and the role of National Socialism in the history of twentieth-century Europe. . . .
   This view leads to an overwhelming concentration on the sequence of diplomatic events, and a failure to see German foreign policy in the
35 general context of National Socialist politics. The foreign policy of the Third Reich was dynamic in character, limitless in its aims to achieve domination and entirely lacking a conception of an 'ultimate *status quo*'. This expansionist drive was the unique contribution of National Socialism, and the feature which most clearly distinguishes Hitler's
40 foreign policy from that of his predecessors. In concentrating the reader's attention on the detailed circumstances which enabled Germany to make territorial gains prior to the outbreak of war, Mr Taylor omits a satisfactory analysis of the mainsprings of German policy. Expansionism is sometimes taken for granted, sometimes represented merely as the
45 restoration of German power in Europe or as the revision of Versailles, and is sometimes dismissed adverbially; it is never assigned any definite role among the causes of the Second World War.
   This weakness is due in part to Mr Taylor's abrupt dismissal of 'the cloud of phrases' which enveloped German policy, his refusal to accept
50 that policy was in any way determined by the ideology or by the internal political structure of the Third Reich. . . .
   This is the historical context in which Hitler's personal characteristics must be seen; the facility with which he resorted to force or the threat of force in international affairs, his need to achieve success after success in
55 foreign policy were not minor contingent factors on the European scene, but basic traits of the political movement which he led.
   The second thesis seems equally open to question: 'My book really has little to do with Hitler. The vital question, it seems to me, concerns Great Britain and France. They were the victors of the First World War. They
60 had the decision in their hands.' Mr Taylor has clearly shown that in the individual crises which led up to the outbreak of war in 1939, many important initiatives came from Britain and France, but this is insufficient

evidence that his general perspective is the right one. In the Europe of the 1930s the Third Reich was the most potent force for change — for change in boundaries no less than for change in political and economic techniques or social and cultural values. Mr Taylor insists that 'the crisis of March 1938 was provoked by Schuschnigg', and that the crisis which culminated in the Munich Settlement was 'of British making', and he lays some emphasis on the fact that President Hacha of Czechoslovakia was not summoned to Berlin in March 1939 but asked to come of his own accord. In doing so he omits to ask why it was possible for these crises to arise at all — why Schuschnigg thought it necessary to call a plebiscite in Austria, why in the late spring of 1938, 'Everyone in Europe felt [that] . . . the Czechoslovak round was due to begin', why Hacha saw no alternative but to turn to Hitler. It is a question of perspective; in a longer perspective the initiatives of other governments appear rather as responses to problems raised by Nazi Germany. Crucial decisions were certainly made in all the capitals of Europe, but the Third Reich determined what it was the victor powers had to decide about. The fact that the Sudetenland and Danzig arose at all as *acute, international* problems was due almost exclusively to the hegemony of the National Socialist party within Germany. In rightly insisting that the expansionist aims of the Reich were at no stage formulated into a comprehensive plan, Mr Taylor wrongly conveys the impression that they were of little importance. . . .

The fundamental argument of Mr Taylor's book is that it takes two to make a war; more accurately, that it took Britain and France to make a European war. It does not really explain why the Third Reich was willing to risk a European war. . . .

Mr Taylor's judgements rest very largely upon the diplomatic documents. . . . these documents were primarily the work of conservative German diplomats, who, in dealing with their specific problems, were able to cover up or ignore the distinctive language and concepts of National Socialism. This helps to nurture the illusion that the foreign policy of the Third Reich was much the same as that of the Weimar Republic, and that it served the same functional purposes as the foreign policies of the other powers.

Neither do the documents give an adequate picture of the role of the Nazi movement inside Austria and Czechoslovakia; their movements are portrayed as the objects of diplomacy, and Mr Taylor tends to reflect this emphasis. Thus he adduces the existence of a militant pro-Nazi movement among the Sudeten Germans as further proof that Hitler did not initiate the crisis over Czechoslovakia. Though the point is illuminating in a sense, it encourages the making of too radical a distinction between Hitler the German statesman and Hitler the leader of the Nazi movement. The persistent and violent disruption of ordered life in Austria and Czechoslovakia was a crucial contribution of National Socialism to pre-war international relations. It severely weakened the internal structure of both states, created an atmosphere of continual crisis and in the latter case provided Hitler with the indispensable pretext of

110 self-determination; . . . In short, the National Socialist movement created conditions in which the actual course of events in Central Europe was made very probable, if not fully predetermined. And the fact that the Austrian and the Sudeten parties often acted independently of the German leadership indicates in the first instance the central role of the

115 movement in the history of the period; Hitler's opportunism is only meaningful within this context. The question 'why' cannot be asked of the diplomatic documents alone. . . .

. . . the Hossbach Protocol remains of vital interest to the student of German foreign policy, but the importance of the conference must first

120 be demonstrated before valid conclusions can be drawn from the document. Of the practical effects of Hitler's monologue, Mr Taylor writes, 'There was here . . . no directive for German policy'; and, 'At the time, no one attached importance to the meeting.' In the middle of December, seven weeks after the conference, the mobilisation orders of

125 the armed forces were changed; the orders of July 1937 envisaged a preventive German invasion of Czechoslovakia in the events of Franco–Russian aggression against the Reich. Those of December postulated (given favourable international circumstances) German aggression against Austria and Czechoslovakia. This change mirrored the new

130 temper and new aims of Hitler's policy as he had expounded it to his military leaders on 5 November. The conference marks the point at which the expansion of the Third Reich ceased to be latent and became explicit.

T. W. Mason, 'Some Origins of the Second World War', *Past and Present*, Dec. 1964; reprinted in E. M. Robertson (ed.), *The Origins of the Second World War*, 1971, pp 105–6, 108–12, 114

Questions

a   Explain 'the cloud of phrases' (lines 48–9); 'Sudetenland' (line 80); 'Danzig' (line 80); 'hegemony' (line 81).

b   What, in Mason's view, are the main omissions from Taylor's book?

c   How, according to Mason, did National Socialism affect Hitler's foreign policy?

d   How does Mason differ from Taylor on the part played by other European leaders in events from 1936 to 1939?

e   What contribution is made on the value of the Hossbach Memorandum [Protocol]? Why does Mason consider the available diplomatic documents inadequate on their own?

*   f   Do the criticisms by Mason seriously undermine the validity of Taylor's book?

5   Profound Causes and Specific Events

. . . it is necessary to uncover two other errors in logic which are closely related and which enter directly into his treatment of those events. Just as his interpretation of the crises that began in 1936 is central to the doubt he casts, at the beginning of the book, on the almost universal view that Hitler 'planned the Second World War', that 'his will alone caused it', so it is central to his analysis of these crises that in no case was German policy the cause of them. All that his evidence can be strained to yield, on the most generous of conditions, is that German *planning* did not actually *occasion* these crises. He never sees the difference between general policy and precise planning or between cause and occasion . . . [while] he dwells not on Hitler's aims or on his policy or even on his 'projections' in his discussion of the crises, but only on Hitler's lack of precise plans. . . .

. . . Because of his confusion of plans with policy and of occasion with cause, Mr Taylor's version of the pre-war crises is devoid of all regard for the policy of the man who almost wholly caused them on one level. . . . It cannot be too much emphasised that, while the profound causes lie among the given conditions that invite war, the causes on the other level are not simply events. They are the ways in which men handle events, react to the challenge which the given conditions present to them. . . . A war is always an alternative to some other course and is always known to be so. . . . Mr Taylor's analysis of these crises is insulated not only from all regard for the policy of the man who almost wholly caused them on one level but also . . . from all recollection of the extreme international unbalance that was the chief cause for them on the other. . . . The unbalance was so much the cause of Hitler's policy that anyone else in power in Germany might have had a policy similar to Hitler's at least in its objects. It was so much the cause of war that, while it was practically impossible for other Powers to resist Germany's revisionist attitude up to and including the Munich crisis, and equally impossible that they should not resist it if it were persisted in much beyond that point, it set up the danger that it would be so persisted in. But it does not much advance the cause of historical truth to assert that Hitler was not responsible because somebody else in the same position might have pursued the same course; or to assume that anyone else must have pursued it beyond the Munich crisis, when the risks had become so great and so obvious. What we do know is that Hitler did pursue it beyond that point. And what we can conclude from any objective analysis of the pre-war crises is that it was this fact, not the unbalance itself that caused the war. . . . The most that the evidence will allow us to say is that Hitler involved himself and Europe in war in spite of all his hopes — but because of his refusal to modify his policy of exploiting the international unbalance for aggressive ends.

F. H. Hinsley, *Power and the Pursuit of Peace: Theory and Practice in the History of Relations between States*, 1963, pp 328–34

Questions

a   What light does Hinsley throw on the discussion of 'aims' and 'plans'?
b   What is the distinction between 'occasion' and 'cause'?
c   What criticism of Taylor is contained in this extract: 'the

causes . . . are not simply events. They are the ways in which men handle events . . .' (lines 17–19)?

* d What was the 'extreme international unbalance' (line 24) in the inter-war period?

  e Where does Hinsley see Hitler's responsibility in the crises of 1937–9?

* f Why is it too simplistic for Taylor to say that '[Hitler] exploited events far more than he followed precise coherent plans'?

Further Work

a A stimulating debate on German rearmament and the drive towards autarky was precipitated by Taylor's book. To what extent did Taylor misuse research on this subject, as suggested by Mason, Carr and others? What was the role of *Blitzkrieg* warfare, and how did this affect Germany's rearmament and foreign policy from 1936?

b '. . . Western statesmen mistook a fundamental irrationalism and limitlessness of policy for an unscrupulousness of method and technique, enlisted, as it seemed, for bargaining purposes.' (A. Adamthwaite) Was this problem of perception (as in the rise of Nazism) fundamental in the failure of appeasement in the late 1930s?

c Is there continuity in German foreign policy from Bismarck to Hitler? Is this implied in Taylor's comment, 'In international affairs there was nothing wrong with Hitler except that he was a German'?

d 'Adolf Hitler had made his aims in foreign policy quite clear in *Mein Kampf*. . . .' (J. Joll) Discuss this statement with reference to Chapter 14 of *Mein Kampf*.

IX   Misunderstanding and Suspicions – The Cold War

Introduction

The question of definition is of crucial importance for the historian. Yet defining a period is no easy matter. This is particularly the case with the chronology of the Cold War. Some historians have claimed that the Cold War began with the Bolshevik Revolution in 1917, while others prefer 1947 as its starting point. Its terminal date is also a matter of considerable discussion. Some writers believe that it is still being waged and that *détente* is merely a Cold War in a less obvious form. This chapter is concerned with the developments of the immediate post-war period and looks at the increase in tension following the defeat of the common enemy.

The historian is faced with one major problem in any objective attempt at analysing the Cold War, the difficulty of obtaining Soviet sources for the period. As a result the contemporary documents in this chapter are exclusively western, and in that sense put forward a one-sided view. Just how biased that view is, the individual must himself decide.

The Yalta conference early in 1945 marked the high-point of allied co-operation and also the beginning of the post-war conflicts. The defeat of the Axis powers could not be long delayed by this time and the question of how Europe was to be organised became an issue of paramount importance. The Yalta Declaration shows what the Three Powers saw as the theory behind post-war reconstruction. It is perhaps best seen as a diplomatic necessity; even a simple consideration of Soviet ideology would have demonstrated its inoperable character to the western powers. Churchill's telegram of May 1945 to President Truman shows the increasing suspicion felt by Britain over the actions of Russia with 'their misinterpretation of the Yalta decisions . . .'. Is Churchill posing the question of some military operation against Russia?

By 1946 the relations between the West and Russia had further deteriorated. The last great conference of the Allies at Potsdam in August 1945 saw Stalin taking advantage of the less experienced Truman and Attlee; on a number of questions, he presented them with a fait accompli. Truman's letter to James Byrnes makes clear the ways in which the West viewed. Soviet imperialism. This view was made more explicit by Churchill in his 'iron curtain' speech at Fulton in March 1946.

The reasons for this deterioration in relations between the West and Russia lie in misunderstandings and suspicions on both sides. Martin Wight's analysis of the post-war settlement is based very much on the idea of balance of power which, as he saw it, Stalin was attempting to upset. Walter Laquer provides a more balanced analysis of this period taking into account the revisionist historians of the 1960s. He argues that the declining relations were a consequence, on the one hand, of the necessities of the Soviet state which needed 'tension not relaxation' to survive; and, on the other, of the disillusion of Europe and the filling of the vacuum so created by the Americans – the *raison d'être* of their policy of containment.

The Cold War was a 'war' with only one defined objective, that of preventing the other side obtaining too much influence. It had, however, the character of a crusade or jihad. That it has not heated up is a consequence not of unwillingness to fight but of unwillingness to use nuclear and atomic weapons. The balance of terror has replaced the balance of power as *the* dominant force in relations between East and West.

Further Reading

S. E. Ambrose, *Rise to Globalism – American Foreign Policy 1938–1976*, Penguin, 1976, a good, brief analysis of the question from the American viewpoint.

* D. F. Fleming, *The Cold War and Its Origins 1917–1960*, 2 vols, Allen & Unwin, 1961, a good, if badly organised study which is highly critical of American policy.

H. Higgins, *The Cold War*, Heinemann, 1974, a good introductory book.

W. LaFeber, *America, Russia and the Cold War*, Wiley, New York, 1967, a shorter and much more balanced book than Fleming's study.

A. B. Ulam, *Expansion and Co-existence*, Secker and Warburg, 1975, a study of Russian foreign policy since 1917.

1 Post-war Europe – the Theory

The following declaration has been approved:

'The Premier of the Union of Soviet Socialist Republics, the Prime Minister of the United Kingdom and the President of the United States of America have consulted with each other in the common interests of the
5 people of their countries and those of liberated Europe. They jointly declare their mutual agreement to concert during the temporary period of instability in liberated Europe the policies of their three governments in assisting the peoples liberated from the domination of Nazi Germany and the peoples of the former Axis satellite states of Europe to solve by
10 democratic means their pressing political and economic problems.

'The establishment of order in Europe and the re-building of national economic life must be achieved by processes which will enable the liberated peoples to destroy the last vestiges of Nazism and Fascism and to create democratic institutions of their own choice. This is a principle of the Atlantic Charter – the right of all peoples to choose the form of government under which they will live – the restoration of sovereign rights and self-government to those peoples who have been forcibly deprived of them by the aggressor nations.

'To foster the conditions in which the liberated peoples may exercise these rights, the three governments will jointly assist the people in any European liberated state or former Axis satellite state in Europe where in their judgment conditions require (a) to establish conditions of internal peace; (b) to carry out emergency measures for the relief of distressed peoples; (c) to form interim governmental authorities broadly representative of all democratic elements in the population and pledged to the earliest possible establishment through free elections of governments responsive to the will of the people; and (d) to facilitate where necessary the holding of such elections.

'The three governments will consult the other United Nations and provisional authorities or other governments in Europe when matters of direct interest to them are under consideration.

' . . . By this declaration we reaffirm our faith in the principles of the Atlantic Charter, our pledge in the Declaration by the United Nations, and our determination to build in co-operation with other peace-loving nations world order under law, dedicated to peace, security, freedom and general well-being of all mankind.

'In issuing this declaration, the Three Powers express the hope that the Provisional Government of the French Republic may be associated with them in the procedure suggested.'

> From the Yalta Conference Protocol: Declaration on liberated Europe, 11 February 1945; U.S. Department of State, *Foreign Relations of the United States, The Conference at Malta and Yalta, 1945*, 1955, pp 977–8

Questions

a (i) Who were the 'Premier of the Union of Soviet Socialist Republics' (line 2); 'Prime Minister of the United Kingdom' (lines 2–3); 'President of the United States of America' (lines 3–4); 'peoples liberated from the domination of Nazi Germany and the peoples of the former Axis Satellite states of Europe' (lines 8–9)?

(ii) What was 'the Atlantic Charter' (line 15) and why was it important?

(iii) What is meant by 'the restoration of sovereign rights' (lines 16–17)?

(iv) What do lines 24–7 mean and why was this to be the main stumbling block to co-operation between East and West?

(v) What were 'the other United Nations' (line 29)?

b Why was the conference at Yalta held? What did it achieve?

c What does this document imply that the responsibilities of Soviet Russia, Britain and America would be in the immediate post-war period?

d The Yalta Protocol was an example of diplomatic necessity. Its principles were to be inoperable in practice. Why?

* e For many peoples liberation meant the replacement of one totalitarian régime by another. Discuss.

2 Divisions Emerge

. . . I am profoundly concerned about the European situation. I learn that half the American Air Force in Europe has already begun to move to the Pacific theatre. The newspapers are full of the great movement of the American armies out of Europe. Our armies also are, under previous
5 arrangements, likely to undergo marked reduction. The Canadian Army will certainly leave. The French are weak and difficult to deal with. Anyone can see that in a very short space of time our armed power on the Continent will have vanished, except for moderate forces to hold down Germany.

10 2. Meanwhile what is to happen about Russia? I have always worked for friendship with Russia, but, like you, I feel deep anxiety because of their misinterpretation of the Yalta decisions, their attitudes towards Poland, their overwhelming influence in the Balkans, excepting Greece, the difficulties they make about Vienna, the combination of Russian
15 power and the territories under their control or occupied, coupled with the Communist technique in so many other countries, and above all their power to maintain very large armies in the field for a long time. What will be the position in a year or two, when the British and American Armies have melted . . . and when Russia may choose to keep two or
20 three hundred [divisions] on active service?

3. An iron curtain is drawn down upon their front. We do not know what is going on behind. There seems little doubt that the whole of the regions east of the line Lübeck—Trieste—Corfu will soon be completely in their hands. To this must be added the further enormous area
25 conquered by the American armies between Eisenach and the Elbe, which will, I suppose, in a few weeks be occupied, when the Americans retreat, by the Russian power. All kinds of arrangements will have to be made by General Eisenhower to prevent another immense flight of the German population westwards as this enormous Muscovite advance into
30 the centre of Europe takes place. . . . Thus a broad band of many hundreds of miles of Russian-occupied territory will isolate us from Poland.

4. Meanwhile the attention of our peoples will be occupied in inflicting severities upon Germany, which is ruined and prostrate, and it
35 would be open to the Russians in a very short time to advance if they chose to the waters of the North Sea and the Atlantic.

5. Surely it is vital now to come to an understanding with Russia . . . before we weaken our armies mortally or retire to the zones of occupation. . . . To sum up, this issue of the settlement with Russia
40 before our strength has gone seems to me to dwarf all others.

Telegram from Winston Churchill to Harry Truman, 12 May 1945; in Winston S. Churchill, *The Second World War*, vol VI, 1954, pp 498–9

Questions

a (i)   What did Churchill mean by 'the Pacific theatre' (lines 2–3)?
   (ii) Churchill said 'I have always worked for friendship with Russia' (lines 10–11). How true was this?
   (iii) In what ways did the Russians misinterpret 'the Yalta decisions' and what were their 'attitudes toward Poland' (lines 12–13)?
   (iv) What do you think Churchill meant by 'the Communist technique' (line 16)?
   (v)   What did the area 'between Eisenach and the Elbe' (line 25) become? Were Churchill's fears well-founded on this issue?
   (vi) Who was General Eisenhower (line 28)?
b Who were Winston Churchill and Harry Truman and what were their rôles during the Second World War?
c What does this telegram tell you about Churchill's attitude towards Russia?
d The emphasis in the telegram was placed by Churchill on the implications of weakening military forces in Europe. Was his assessment of the results of this move borne out in the 1945 to 1953 period?
* e Why was the question of Poland so important in the immediate post-war period?

3 The Rubicon Appears

. . . I think we ought to protest with all the vigor of which we are capable against the Russia program in Iran. There is no justification for it. It is parallel to the program of Russia in Latvia, Estonia and Lithuania. It is also in line with the high-handed and arbitrary manner in which Russia
5 acted in Poland.

At Potsdam we were faced with an accomplished fact and were by circumstances almost forced to agree to the Russian occupation of Eastern Poland and the occupation of that part of Germany east of the Oder River by Poland. It was a high-handed outrage.
10 At the time we were anxious for Russian entry into the Japanese War. Of course we found later that we didn't need Russia there and that the Russians have been a headache to us ever since.

When you went to Moscow you were faced with another accomplished fact in Iran. Another outrage if ever I saw one.

15 Iran was our ally in the war. Iran was Russia's ally in the war. Iran agreed to the free passage of arms, ammunition and other supplies running into million of tons across her territory from the Persian Gulf to the Caspian Sea. Without these supplies furnished by the United States, Russia would have been ignominiously defeated. Yet now Russia stirs up

20 rebellion and keeps troops on the soil of her friend and ally – Iran.

There isn't any doubt in my mind that Russia intends an invasion of Turkey and the seizure of the Black Sea Straits to the Mediterranean. Unless Russia is faced with an iron fist and strong language another war is in the making. Only one language do they understand – 'How many

25 divisions have you?'

I do not think we should play compromise any more. We should refuse to recognize Romania and Bulgaria until they comply with our requirements; we should let our position on Iran be known in no uncertain terms and we should continue to insist on the inter-

30 nationalization of the Kiel Canal, the Rhine–Danube waterway and the Black Sea Straits and we should maintain complete control of Japan and the Pacific. We should rehabilitate China and create a strong central government there. We should do the same for Korea.

Then we should insist on the return of our ships from Russia and force

35 a settlement of the Lend–Lease debt of Russia.

I'm tired of babying the Soviets.

> Letter from President Truman to Secretary of State James Byrnes,
> 5 January 1946, in W. Hillman, *Mr President*, 1952

Questions

a   (i)   What was 'the Russia program in Iran' (line 2)? Why was Iran important to both East and West?

(ii)   What happened at Potsdam in 1945?

(iii)   Why did America find that they 'didn't need Russia' (line 11) in the Japanese War?

(iv)   What are 'the Black Sea Straits' (line 22) and why did Truman fear their seizure by Russia?

(v)   Explain the reference to China (lines 32–3)

*   b   Who was James Byrnes and what part did he play in the diplomacy of the post-war period?

c   Why was Truman more willing to take a stand over the position of Russia in Iran but less willing over the Baltic states and Poland?

d   What does this letter tell you of Truman's attitude towards Russia in early 1946?

*   e   This letter exemplifies Truman's complete lack of any diplomatic sense. He misunderstood or failed to understand Russian intentions. Truman must be viewed as largely responsible for the Cold War. Discuss.

4 The Curtain's Drawn

. . . A shadow has fallen upon the scenes so lately lightened by the Allied victory. Nobody knows what Soviet Russia and its Communist international organization intends to do in the immediate future, or what are the limits, if any, to their expansive and proselytising tendencies. I
5 have a strong admiration and regard for the valiant Russian people and for my war-time comrade, Marshal Stalin. There is sympathy and goodwill in Britain − and, I doubt not, here also − towards the peoples of all the Russias, and a resolve to persevere through many differences and rebuffs in establishing lasting friendships. We understand the Russian
10 need to be secure on her western frontiers from all renewal of German agression. We welcome her to her rightful place among the leading nations of the world. Above all, we welcome constant, frequent, and growing contacts between the Russian people and our own people on both sides of the Atlantic. It is my duty, however, to place before you
15 certain facts about the present position in Europe.

From Stettin, in the Baltic, to Trieste, in the Adriatic, an iron curtain has descended across the continent. Behind that line lie all the capitals of the ancient States of Central and Eastern Europe − Warsaw, Berlin, Prague, Vienna, Budapest, Belgrade, Bucharest and Sofia. All these
20 famous cities . . . are subject in one form or another, not only to Soviet influence, but to a very high and increasing measure of control from Moscow. Athens alone, with its immortal glories, is free to decide its future at an election under British, American and French observation. The Polish Government has been encouraged to make enormous and
25 wrongful inroads upon Germany, and mass expulsions of millions of Germans on a scale grievous and undreamed of are now taking place. The Communist Parties, which were very small in all these Eastern States of Europe, have been raised to pre-eminence and power far beyond their numbers, and are seeking everywhere to obtain totalitarian control.
30 Police governments are prevailing in nearly every case, and so far, except in Czechoslovakia, there is no true democracy. Turkey and Persia are both profoundly alarmed and disturbed at the claims which are made upon them and at the pressure being exerted by the Moscow Government. An attempt is being made by the Russians in Berlin to build
35 up a quasi-Communist party in their zone of occupation by showing special favours to groups of Left-wing German leaders.

. . . Whatever conclusions may be drawn from these facts − and facts they are − this is certainly not the liberated Europe we fought to build up. Nor is it one which contains the essentials of permanent peace.

From the 'iron curtain' speech made by Winston Churchill at Fulton, Missouri on 5 March 1946; in W. S. Churchill, *Sinews of Peace: Post-War Speeches*, p 94

Questions

a (i) What did Churchill mean by 'its Communist international organization' (lines 2−3); 'totalitarian control' (line 29) and 'true democracy' (line 31)?

(ii) Churchill referred to the needs of the Russians 'to be secure on her western frontiers' (line 10). How did Russia achieve security?

(iii) How far was there 'a very high and increasing measure of control from Moscow' (lines 21−2) over eastern Europe?

(iv) Explain the reference to Poland in lines 24−5.

b How effective do you think Churchill's speech was as a piece of oratory?

* *c* The Fulton speech was misunderstood by both the West and Russia. The West saw it as a call to arms, the East as a threat to what they saw as their rightful position in eastern Europe. In fact it was neither of these. It was a statement of facts. Discuss.

5 Post-War Settlement?

. . . The peace conferences at the end of general wars had steadily grown more comprehensive; and resembled the great legislative gatherings of international society. Now they ceased. In 1946 there was a diminutive Paris Peace Conference, which made treaties between twenty-one chief
5 Allied powers and the minor enemy states of Europe – Italy, Hungary, Rumania, Bulgaria and Finland. A corresponding treaty with Austria was delayed until 1955. But the victorious powers were unable to agree on a peace settlement with their two principal enemies. With Japan, the United states and forty-seven of her associates signed a peace treaty at San
10 Francisco in 1951; but this was rejected by the Communist powers, India and Burma, and was signed by neither Chinese government since the Western powers could not decide which of these ought to be represented. Russia made peace separately with Japan in 1956. With Germany, a peace treaty was impossible, in the Western view, until Germany was reunited;
15 and the reunification of Germany was the most intractable of all post-war diplomatic problems. The economic success of federal Germany, and her adoption into the defensive system of the Western powers, seem to show that a peace treaty can be dispensed with. But the chronic weakness of the Eastern Germany, the Russian need to give this satellite power
20 some legal status, the unconfirmed frontier between Eastern Germany and Poland, and above all the dangerous and anomalous position of West Berlin, were directly connected with the absence of a peace treaty.
. . . Victorious allies had always in the past fallen apart when the danger from the common enemy had been removed, but never before had
25 conflict between the victorious allies broken out so quickly and implacably: another sign of the general deterioration in international relations. For the cold war was only a new phase of the doctrinal conflict between Bolshevik Russia and the rest of the world that had gone on

since 1917. . . . Western fear and hatred of Communism had been seen
when Russia was expelled from the League for her attack on Finland in
December 1939, a punishment not inflicted on Japan or Italy for their
aggressions. Soviet distrust of the West had been seen throughout the
diplomacy of the Second World War. . . .

On the Russian side, the beginnings of the cold war were perhaps seen
in a suspicion that the Western powers were in collusion with the
Germans during the last months of the war, in the abrupt and unfriendly
ending of Lend-Lease by the United States in the summer of 1945, and in
the dropping of two atomic bombs on Japan, which showed that the
United States no longer needed the Soviet help in defeating Japan that
had been promised at Yalta, and that she had suddenly acquired a new and
vast military superiority over her exhausted ally. On the Western side,
they were seen in the ruthlessness and chicanery with which Stalin
imposed a Communist government on Poland. The first effect of the cold
war was the division of Europe and the Middle East between the Soviet
and Western blocs. The states of Eastern Europe, which had been
conquered or reduced to satellites by Nazi Germany, were now swiftly
Communized by Russia. Czechoslovakia maintained a precarious balance between East and West under Benes; and Greece, a Mediterranean
not a Balkan state, which had been liberated by the British, had a
conservative royalist regime. Russia pushed heavily against her southern
frontier. . . . The United States replied in 1947 with the Truman
Doctrine, the first example of the policy of containment, which advanced
American lines of defence to embrace Greece and Turkey, promising
them the aid Britain had become too weak to give. Three months later
the United States took the diplomatic initiative with the Marshall
Plan. . . . Russia rejected the Marshall Plan for herself and for her
satellites, thus demonstrating the division of Europe; and the Marshall
Plan became, what perhaps its authors had wanted it to be, a revival of the
economies of Western Europe under American guidance, and a move in
the policy of containment.

Russia retaliated in September 1947 by establishing the
Cominform. . . . She also destroyed the coalition government in Prague
in 1948 and imposed Communism on Czechoslovakia, which had
wanted to accept the Marshall Plan and had been compelled to reverse her
policy in a humiliating manner. This violent coup . . . hastened the
establishment of Western Union between Britain, France, Belgium,
Holland and Luxembourg by the Brussels Treaty of March 1948. . . . A
year later they were joined by the United States in the North Atlantic
Treaty Organization. . . . This was the first alliance formed in time of
peace providing for an organized military force. . . .

These developments were reflected and exaggerated in the mirror of
Germany. . . . Russia's ultimate goal was probably to transform a united
Germany into a Communist satellite (Germany had once had the largest
and strongest Communist Party in the world). The West's ultimate goal
was to re-educate Germany into a law-abiding and democratic member

of international society, who might freely choose to cooperate with the West against Communism. . . . The Marshall Plan stimulated the Americans and British to fuse their zones of occupation so that German industry might contribute to European recovery. . . . Russia retaliated
80 by stopping land communication between Western Germany and Western Berlin. The Berlin blockade was a bloodless battle, waged from June 1948 to May 1949, and won by the airlift and a counter-blockade of the Eastern Zone. The raising of the blockade, and the ending of the guerilla war in Greece the same autumn, marked the failure of the
85 Russian attempt to alter the *status quo post bellum* in Europe. Germany was now irretrievably divided. . . . The balance of power in Europe, created when the Soviet and Western armies met in the heart of defeated Germany in May 1945, and endangered by the rapid demobilization of the Western powers, had been restored.

> M. Wight, *Power Politics*, ed. by Hedley Bull and Carsten
> Holbraad, 1979, pp 219−24

Questions

a (i) What is the meaning of the following: 'federal Germany' (line 16); 'Lend-Lease' (line 37); 'Yalta' (line 40); 'the Truman Doctrine' (lines 51−2); 'the Marshall Plan' (lines 55−6); 'the Cominform' (line 62); 'zones of occupation' (line 78)?

(ii) What does Wight mean when he talked of 'neither Chinese government' (line 11)?

(iii) Why was a peace treaty with Germany impossible in the Western view (lines 13−14)?

(iv) Why was the position of West Berlin 'dangerous and anomalous' (lines 21−2)?

(v) Explain the reference to the 'doctrinal conflict. . . .' (lines 27−8).

(vi) How were 'The states of Eastern Europe . . . swiftly Communized by Russia' (lines 45−7)?

(vii) Why is Greece viewed as 'a Mediterranean not a Balkan state' (lines 48−9)?

(viii) What does 'the *status quo post bellum*' (line 85) mean?

* *b* In what ways did the peace conferences of the twentieth century resemble 'the great legislative gatherings of international society' (lines 2−3)?

c How does Wight see mutual suspicion developing between Russia and the West in the immediate post-war years?

* *d* How accurate do you think Wight's balance of power thesis is as a tool for examining the Cold War?

e How far were the problems of the post-war period 'reflected and exaggerated in the mirror of Germany'? (lines 71−2)

6 Revisionism – the Move Towards Synthesis

Protestant and Catholic rulers in Europe had agreed after the Reformation on the principle that the religion professed by the individual should depend on his place of residence: *cujus regio – ejus religio.* Could an arrangement on similar lines have worked in post-war Europe? Stalin
5 seems to have thought so; he said on one occasion that this war was different from previous ones inasmuch as the occupying power was imposing its social system on the countries under its control. . . . It was doubtful whether any such arrangement would have worked in central Europe, even if America had accepted the principle of spheres of interest.
10 Communism was ideologically committed to renew the struggle against 'Western Imperialism' once the war ended. . . . The renewal of the contest could have been delayed but not indefinitely postponed. In Stalin's eyes the Western proposals to establish governments that were friendly to the Soviet Union and yet representative of all the democratic
15 elements in the country were a mere trick, a new attempt at capitalist encirclement. Only communists were acceptable to him. . . . Suspicions and misunderstandings played a certain part in the outbreak of the cold war, but below these suspicions there were real conflicts of interest. Collaboration with the West after 1945 would have involved the
20 liberalization of Stalin's régime and the opening of the Soviet Union to all kinds of undesirable foreign influences. . . . During the war, when his country was threatened, certain conditions had to be made, but the continuation of such policies in peacetime would have endangered the very existence of the Soviet state. This was Stalin's basic
25 dilemma. . . . His political system was based on state-of-siege mentality; the sacrifices he demanded from his people could be justified only with reference to the unrelenting hostility of the capitalist wolves and sharks waiting for the opportunity to attack the Soviet Union. This system needed tension, not relaxation, in its relations with the outside world. . . .
30 Three years after the end of the war Europe's main economic wounds had been healed; industrial and agricultural output had almost reached the prewar level. . . . There were moreover serious difficulties that had not existed before the war . . . [there] was, in fact, a structural crisis, for Europe's place in the world had radically altered. Nor was it certain
35 whether Europe still had the will and the ability to regain its old prosperity and influence. 'What is Europe now?' Churchill wrote in 1947. 'A rubble heap, a charnel house, a breeding ground of pestilence and hate.' He was not alone in his pessimism.

  Within a year of the end of the war the Soviet Union accused its former
40 allies of fascist aggression, imperialist expansion, and preparing a new world war. On the other hand, many people in the West felt . . . that the police governments established in eastern Europe did not represent the liberated Europe they had fought for, nor did such a Europe contain the essentials for peace. Many came to believe with President Truman that

45   unless Russia was met with a strong hand and an iron fist, another world war would be in the making. . . . But who had expected that within two years after the end of hostilities Europe would be divided into two implacably hostile camps, and that there would be widespread fear of a new world war?

50   Western policy during the immediate postwar period has been severely criticized from opposed points of view. Around 1950 the general opinion was that Western policy towards the Soviet Union had been too credulous and soft. A decade later some critics argued, on the contrary, the West had not shown enough goodwill, that there had been hysteria

55   and a tendency to overrate both Soviet hostility and Soviet power. Stalinist Russia, they argued, was basically a conservative country in search of security, but with no desire to expand beyond its natural borders. There is some truth, though not necessarily an equal measure, in both contentions. . . . In 1946 the Greek civil war was resumed from

60   bases beyond Greece's border. The Soviet Union refused to withdraw from Persia and put growing pressure on Turkey. All opposition was gradually eliminated in eastern Europe and the Balkans, while Soviet efforts to impose its political system on its zone of Germany became more intense. At the foreign ministers' meeting throughout 1946–7 little

65   progress was achieved towards a lasting peace settlement. The Soviet stand became more and more adamant, despite constant, often pathetic, Western attempts to reach compromises and to allay Soviet suspicions. In 1947 and 1948 the situation deteriorated further; the democratic régime was overthrown in Czechoslovakia which became a fully-fledged

70   satellite; the Berlin blockade was imposed; the Soviet Union refused to co-operate with the West in the new projects for the economic recovery of Europe . . . and the attempts to establish international control of nuclear weapons. . . . The West felt suddenly cheated, and in this rude awakening many wartime illusions were shattered and there was an

75   inclination to overdramatize the conflict, to attribute to Stalin and the other communist leaders not only satanic cunning and evil but also relentless and unlimited territorial ambitions. Having ignored communist ideology for many years, there was now in the West a growing inclination to take strictly at face value all theoretical writings about

80   world revolution and the coming inevitable struggle. There was a tendency to view largely in military terms a struggle that was essentially political in nature. On these counts Western policy has rightly been criticized. . . . At the height of the cold war the slogan of the liberation of eastern Europe gained some currency in the West, but there was little

85   thought and even less conviction behind it; the posture of the West was essentially defensive; it had little to oppose to the dynamic, aggressive policy of the Soviet Union and the communist parties. There were foolish speeches and irresponsible actions on the part of Western leaders which aggravated relations with the Soviet Union, and some of the fears

90   were quite irrational. . . . The cold war created a far greater degree of European unity that had been thought possible, and it also brought about

lasting American involvement in European affairs. These developments were highly undesirable from the Soviet point of view, and to that extent Soviet policy between 1946 and 1949 can be said to have failed. Soviet influence in Europe was no longer expanding; the borders were frozen, and a stalemate prevailed in international relations. . . .

The cold war was a contest without victors. Forced on the West, it had retarded and distorted its social and political development. . . . If the policy of containment was part successful, it was due less to Western farsightedness and determination than to the development of nuclear weapons which revolutionized the risks of war and thus caused a general freeze up of frontiers and of political and social structures.

W. Laquer, *Europe Since Hitler*, 1972, pp 116—21, 128

Questions

a (i) What does the author mean by the following words: 'the principle of spheres of interest' (line 9); 'capitalist encirclement' (lines 15—16); 'Europe's main economic wounds' (line 30); 'police governments' (line 42); 'the Berlin blockade' (line 70); 'the policy of containment' (line 99).

   (ii) In what ways was the Second World War 'different from previous ones . . . under its control' (lines 5—7)?

   (iii) In what ways was the Stalinist system 'based on state-of-siege mentality' (line 26)?

   (iv) Explain why 'The Soviet Union refused . . . Turkey' (lines 60—1)?

   (v) Why was there 'a tendency to view largely . . . political in nature' (lines 80—2)?

* *b* Why does Laquer refer to the Reformation in lines 1—3? What similarities were there between the problems created by the Reformation and the Cold War?

  c Why did continued co-operation with the West put the whole political structure in jeopardy?

* *d* Was there a 'structural crisis' for Europe over its position in the world in the immediate post-war period (line 33)?

  e Laquer puts forward several alternative explanations for the causes of the Cold War. What are they? How satisfactory do you find them?

* *f* The Cold War was a consequence of lack of political understanding by both the Soviet Union and the USA as to the objectives of the other. Discuss.

Further Work

a The Cold War in the immediate post-war period was an extension of the pre-war ideological conflict. Discuss.

b The tension of the post-war period was heightened by mutual misunderstanding and suspicion. These were the motive forces behind the Cold War. Discuss.

c The Cold War threatened to upset the concept of the 'balance of power'. Why?

d Once the question of eastern Europe had been settled it was inevitable that conflict between East and West should centre on Germany and its future. Does this statement help to explain the relationships between West and East between 1946 and 1953?

e *Détente* is just the Cold War under a new heading. Do you agree?